Better Homes and Gardens®

slow
cooker
family dinners

JG
PRESS

Published by World Publications Group, Inc., 140 Laurel Street, East Bridgewater, MA 02333, www.wrldpub.net

Library of Congress Cataloging-in-Publication Data

Slow cooker family dinners.
    p. cm.
  Cover title: At head of title: Better homes and gardens slow cooker family dinners
  Includes index.
  ISBN 978-1-57215-627-2 (cloth) -- ISBN 978-1-57215-632-6 (pbk.)
  1. Electric cookery, Slow. 2. Dinners and dining. I. Better homes and gardens. II. Title: Better homes and gardens slow cooker family dinners.
  TX827.S5527 2010
  641.5'884--dc22
                                            2010019585

Printed in China.

10 9 8 7 6 5 4 3 2 1

Better Homes and Gardens®

Test Kitchen™

Our seal assures you that every recipe in *Slow Cooker Family Dinners* has been tested in the Better Homes and Gardens Test Kitchen®. This means that each recipe is practical and reliable and meets our high standards of taste appeal. We guarantee your satisfaction with this book for as long as you own it.

contents

Slow-Cooker Basics 6

Easy Appetizers 8

Savory Meats and Poultry 36

Effortless Soups and Stews 136

Sumptuous Sides 170

Delicious Desserts 206

Metric Information 234

Index 235

slow-cooker **basics**

With the help of a slow cooker, you can serve hearty, home-style meals whenever you like. Keep these practical pointers in mind to make the most of this versatile, timesaving appliance.

Types of Slow Cookers

When you shop for a slow cooker, you'll find two types—continuous and multipurpose. The recipes in this book were tested with a continuous slow cooker. It has heating coils that wrap around the sides of the unit (see photo, below) and remain on when the cooker is in operation. Usually there are two fixed heat settings—low (about 200°F) and high (about 300°F). Some models also have an automatic setting that shifts from high to low during use. Many models have removable liners.

Multipurpose slow cookers have heating elements located below the food containers and dials that indicate cooking temperatures. Because these units cycle on and off, the recipes in this book will not cook properly in these cookers.

What Size Is Best?

The size of slow cooker you need depends on the number of people you plan to serve. That's why some cooks own several sizes. For one or two servings, the small 1½-quart size works best. It's also handy for keeping appetizers and dips warm at parties. The intermediate 3½- to 4½-quart cooker typically simmers enough to serve three or four. If you have a larger family of five to seven people or want to cook enough for two meals, look for a 4½- or 5-quart cooker. And if you frequently cook for eight or more, you may want to invest in a 6- to 8-quart model.

Avoid Switching Sizes

If you don't have the size of slow cooker called for in a recipe, it's important not to substitute a smaller or larger size. To work most efficiently, a slow cooker must be at least half but no more than two-thirds full. That's because the heat comes from the coils around the sides, not on the bottom. Most of the recipes in this book give a range of cooker sizes (such as 3½- or 4-quart). Be sure to use one that's within the range so the food cooks to the right doneness within the time listed.

Plan Ahead

Because you'll want to start many slow-cooker recipes early in the day, you can eliminate some breakfast-time hassles by preparing ingredients the night before. Here are a few dos and don'ts:

- Chop vegetables and refrigerate them in separate containers.(You can keep cut-up potatoes from turning brown by covering them with water.) Or if your cooker has a removable liner, place the vegetables in the liner, cover it, and keep it in the refrigerator until the next morning.

- Assemble, cover, and chill liquid ingredients or sauces separately from the solids.
- If you'd like to brown ground meat or poultry and bulk sausage the night before, be sure to cook it completely. Then store it tightly covered in the refrigerator. Don't brown roasts, cubed meat, or poultry pieces ahead because browning doesn't cook the meat or poultry completely through.

Adapting Family Recipes
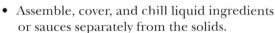

If you'd like to convert a favorite recipe from conventional directions to a slow-cooking method, follow these guidelines:

- Select a recipe that uses a less-tender meat cut, such as pork shoulder or beef chuck, which usually requires long cooking. You'll need to experiment with recipes that use dairy products because they can break down during extended cooking. If you like, stir in cream, sour cream, or cheese just before serving.
- Then find a recipe in this book that's similar to your recipe to use as a sample. It will give you a feel for quantities and liquid amounts.
- Cut vegetables into pieces similar in size to those in the sample recipe; place them in the cooker.
- Trim fat from the meat and, if necessary, cut the meat to fit the cooker. Place it on top of the vegetables.
- Because liquids don't boil away as they do in conventional cooking, reduce the liquids in the original recipe by about half (except those dishes containing rice).
- Follow the heat settings and cooking times listed in the sample recipe.

easy APPETIZERS

Buffalo Wings with Blue Cheese Dip, *recipe page 26*

five-spice PECANS

When you have some of these lively nuts left over, sprinkle them on salads or serve them with fresh pear slices for dessert.

Prep: 10 minutes
Cook: 2 hours (low)
Makes: 16 (¼-cup) servings

 1 **pound pecan halves, toasted***
     (4 cups)
 ¼ **cup butter or margarine,**
     melted
 2 **tablespoons soy sauce**
 1 **teaspoon five-spice powder**
 ½ **teaspoon garlic powder**
 ½ **teaspoon ground ginger**
 ¼ **teaspoon cayenne pepper**

1 Place toasted pecans in a 3½- or 4-quart slow cooker. In a small bowl, combine melted butter, soy sauce, five-spice powder, garlic powder, ginger, and cayenne pepper. Pour butter mixture over nuts in cooker; stir to coat.

2 Cover and cook on low-heat setting for 2 hours.

3 Stir nuts. Spread nuts in a single layer on waxed paper to cool. (Nuts will appear soft after cooking but will crisp upon cooling.) Store in a tightly covered container for up to 2 weeks.

Nutrition facts per serving: 225 cal., 23 g total fat (4 g sat. fat), 8 mg chol., 146 mg sodium, 4 g carbo., 3 g fiber, 3 g pro.

*****Note:** To toast pecans, preheat oven to 350°F. Spread pecans in a single layer on a shallow baking pan. Bake for 5 to 10 minutes or until toasted, stirring once so nuts don't burn.

white BEAN SPREAD

Generally herbs are added at the end of cooking time; however, rosemary can hold up to long cooking. Marjoram is a bit more delicate, so sprinkle more fresh atop the dip before serving.

Prep: 15 minutes
Cook: 3 to 4 hours (low)
Makes: 20 (2-tablespoon) servings

- 2 **15-ounce cans Great Northern or cannellini beans (white kidney beans), rinsed and drained**
- ½ **cup canned chicken or vegetable broth**
- 1 **tablespoon olive oil**
- 3 **cloves garlic, minced**
- 1 **teaspoon snipped fresh marjoram or ¼ teaspoon dried marjoram, crushed**
- ½ **teaspoon snipped fresh rosemary or ⅛ teaspoon dried rosemary, crushed**
- ⅛ **teaspoon ground black pepper**
  Olive oil (optional)
  Fresh marjoram leaves
  Fresh rosemary (optional)
  Pita Chips*

1 In a 1½-quart slow cooker, combine beans, broth, 1 tablespoon oil, garlic, 1 teaspoon snipped marjoram, ½ teaspoon snipped rosemary, and pepper.

2 Cover and cook on low-heat setting for 3 to 4 hours.

3 Slightly mash bean mixture using a potato masher. Spoon bean mixture into a serving bowl. If desired, drizzle with additional oil and sprinkle with fresh marjoram and rosemary. Serve warm or at room temperature with Pita Chips.

***Pita Chips:** Split 2 pita bread rounds horizontally in half; cut each circle into 6 wedges. Place pita wedges in a single layer on a large baking sheet. Combine 2 tablespoons olive oil, 2 teaspoons snipped fresh oregano, and ¼ teaspoon kosher salt; brush pita wedges with oil mixture. Bake in a 350°F oven for 12 to 15 minutes or until crisp and light brown. Remove from baking sheet; cool on a wire rack. Makes 24 chips.

Nutrition facts per serving (spread only): 70 cal., 1 g total fat (0 g sat. fat), 0 mg chol., 33 mg sodium, 11 g carbo., 3 g fiber, 4 g pro.

asiago CHEESE DIP

Yum. Creamy and delicious, this sublime dip is wonderful served on a simple toasted slice of baguette.

Prep: 15 minutes
Cook: 3 to 4 hours (low) or 1½ to
      2 hours (high)
Makes: 28 (¼-cup) servings

  1 **cup chicken broth or water**

  4 **ounces dried tomatoes
     (not oil-packed)**

  4 **8-ounce cartons dairy sour
     cream**

1¼ **cups mayonnaise**

 ½ **of an 8-ounce package cream
     cheese, cut into cubes**

  1 **cup sliced fresh mushrooms**

  1 **cup thinly sliced green
     onions (8)**

1½ **cups shredded Asiago cheese
     (6 ounces)**

     Thinly sliced green onion

     Toasted baguette slices

1 In a medium saucepan, bring broth to boiling. Remove from heat and add dried tomatoes. Cover and let stand for 5 minutes. Drain and discard the liquid; chop tomatoes (about 1¼ cups).

2 Meanwhile, in a 3½- or 4-quart slow cooker, combine sour cream, mayonnaise, cream cheese, mushrooms, 1 cup green onions, and Asiago cheese. Stir in chopped tomatoes. Cover and cook on low-heat setting for 3 to 4 hours or on high-heat setting for 1½ to 2 hours. Stir before serving and sprinkle with additional sliced green onion. Serve immediately or keep warm on low-heat setting for 1 to 2 hours. Serve with toasted baguette slices.

Nutrition facts per serving (dip only): 194 cal., 18 g total fat (8 g sat. fat), 29 mg chol., 237 mg sodium, 5 g carbo., 1 g fiber, 4 g pro.

cheesy BEER-SALSA DIP

Serve this hot dip with dippers made of something unexpected—corn bread. The crunchy sticks are a nice contrast to the spicy dip.

Prep: 15 minutes
Cook: 3 to 4 hours (low) or 1½ to 2 hours (high)
Makes: 22 (¼-cup) servings

- 1 **16-ounce jar salsa**
- ⅔ **cup beer or milk**
- 4 **cups shredded American cheese (1 pound)**
- 2 **cups shredded Monterey Jack cheese (8 ounces)**
- 1 **8-ounce package cream cheese, cut up**

  Corn Bread Dippers* or tortilla chips

1 In a 3½- or 4-quart slow cooker, combine salsa and beer, add American cheese, Monterey Jack cheese, and cream cheese.

2 Cover and cook on low-heat setting for 3 to 4 hours or on high-heat setting for 1½ to 2 hours. Serve immediately or keep covered on low-heat setting for up to 2 hours. Stir just before serving. Serve with Corn Bread Dippers or tortilla chips.

*Corn Bread Dippers: Preheat oven to 400°F. Prepare one 8½-ounce package corn muffin mix according to package directions. Spread batter in an 8x8x2-inch baking pan. Bake for about 20 minutes or until a wooden toothpick inserted in the center comes out clean. Cool bread in pan on a wire rack for 5 minutes. Remove bread from pan; cool completely. Preheat oven to 425°F. Cut into ½-inch-thick slices; cut each slice into 3 pieces. Place in a single layer on a large baking sheet. Bake for about 10 minutes more or until crisp, turning once. Cool on a wire rack. To make ahead, prepare Corn Bread Dippers as directed. Cool sticks completely and store, covered, in an airtight container for up to 2 days.

Nutrition facts per serving (dip only): 211 cal., 15 g total fat (8 g sat. fat), 47 mg chol., 557 mg sodium, 10 g carbo., 0 g fiber, 9 g pro.

spinach-artichoke DIP WITH BLUE CHEESE AND BACON

What's not to like? Smoky bacon and blue cheese are new invitees to this classic dip. One such as this should be part of any top-notch appetizer tray.

Prep: 25 minutes
Cook: 3 to 4 hours (low)
Makes: 24 (¼-cup) servings

- 4 slices bacon
- 1 cup sweet onion, coarsely chopped (1 large)
- 2 14-ounce cans artichoke hearts, drained and coarsely chopped
- 1 10-ounce box frozen chopped spinach, thawed and well drained
- 1 cup chopped red sweet pepper
- 1 cup light mayonnaise dressing (do not use regular mayonnaise)
- 8 ounces cream cheese, cut into cubes
- 4 ounces blue cheese, crumbled
- 3 cloves garlic, minced
- ½ teaspoon dry mustard
  Assorted crackers

1 In a skillet, cook bacon until crisp. Drain on paper towels. Crumble bacon; cover and chill until ready to use. Cook onion in 1 tablespoon bacon drippings for about 5 minutes or until tender.

2 In a 3½- or 4-quart slow cooker, combine onion, artichoke hearts, spinach, red sweet pepper, mayonnaise, cream cheese, blue cheese, garlic, and dry mustard.

3 Cover and cook on low-heat setting for 3 to 4 hours or until cheese melts and mixture is heated through. Stir in bacon. Serve with assorted crackers.

Nutrition facts per serving (dip only): 128 cal., 11 g total fat (4 g sat. fat), 22 mg chol., 341 mg sodium, 4 g carbo., 2 g fiber, 4 g pro.

horseradish-crab DIP

Here's a knockout addition to any appetizer buffet—a cream cheese, mushroom, and crab dip that's perfectly seasoned with horseradish, Worcestershire sauce, and smoky bacon.

Prep: 15 minutes
Cook: 1½ to 2½ hours (low)
Makes: 10 (¼-cup) servings

2 6- or 6.5-ounce cans crabmeat, drained, flaked, and cartilage removed

1 8-ounce package cream cheese, cut into cubes

1 4-ounce can (drained weight) mushroom stems and pieces, drained and chopped

¼ cup finely chopped onion

2 slices bacon, crisp-cooked, drained, and crumbled

2 teaspoons prepared horseradish

1 teaspoon Worcestershire sauce

Rich round crackers and/or celery sticks

1 In a 1½-quart slow cooker, combine crabmeat, cream cheese, mushrooms, onion, bacon, horseradish, and Worcestershire sauce.

2 Cover and cook on low-heat setting for 1½ to 2½ hours. Stir before serving. Serve with crackers and/or celery.

Nutrition facts per serving (dip only): 223 cal., 14 g total fat (6 g sat. fat), 57 mg chol., 426 mg sodium, 14 g carbo., 1 g fiber, 11 g pro.

cajun SPINACH-SHRIMP DIP

Treat your guests to something sensational—serve them this spicy Louisiana-style shrimp dip.

Prep: 15 minutes
Cook: 2 to 3 hours (low)
Makes: 12 (¼-cup) servings

1 **10.75-ounce can condensed cream of shrimp or cream of chicken soup**

1 **10-ounce package frozen chopped spinach, thawed and well drained**

1 **8-ounce package cream cheese, cut into cubes**

1 **4-ounce can tiny shrimp, drained**

¼ **cup finely chopped onion**

¼ **to ½ teaspoon Cajun seasoning**

2 **cloves garlic, minced**
   Celery sticks, sweet pepper strips, and/or crackers

① In a 1½-quart slow cooker, combine cream of shrimp soup, spinach, cream cheese, shrimp, onion, Cajun seasoning, and garlic.

② Cover and cook on low-heat setting for 2 to 3 hours. Stir before serving. Serve with vegetables and/or crackers.

Nutrition facts per serving (dip only): 103 cal., 8 g total fat (5 g sat. fat), 40 mg chol., 290 mg sodium, 4 g carbo., 1 g fiber, 5 g pro.

picadillo DIP

Picadillo is usually a mix of garlic, onion, tomatoes, and meat, but this version mingles in olives, almonds, and raisins for a sophisticated twist.

Prep: 20 minutes
Cook: 6 to 8 hours (low) or 3 to 4 hours (high)
Makes: 16 (¼-cup) servings

- 1 **pound ground beef**
- 1 **16-ounce jar salsa**
- 1 **medium onion, chopped**
- ½ **cup raisins**
- ¼ **cup sliced pimiento-stuffed olives**
- 2 **tablespoons red wine vinegar**
- 3 **cloves garlic, minced**
- ½ **teaspoon ground cinnamon**
- ½ **teaspoon ground cumin**
- ¼ **cup slivered almonds, toasted**
   Slivered almonds, toasted (optional)
   Toasted pita wedges or bagel chips

1 In a large skillet, cook meat until brown. Drain off fat. In a 3½- or 4-quart slow cooker, stir together meat, salsa, onion, raisins, olives, vinegar, garlic, cinnamon, and cumin.

2 Cover and cook on low-heat setting for 6 to 8 hours or on high-heat setting for 3 to 4 hours.

3 Stir the ¼ cup almonds into mixture in cooker. If desired, sprinkle with additional almonds. Serve with toasted pita wedges.

Nutrition facts per serving (dip only): 94 cal., 5 g total fat (2 g sat. fat), 18 mg chol., 217 mg sodium, 7 g carbo., 1 g fiber, 7 g pro.

spicy SAUSAGE PIZZA DIP

If you're lucky enough to have any of this zesty dip left over, spoon it into freezer containers and stash it in the freezer to enjoy later. It will keep for up to 3 months. When you're ready to serve it again, thaw it in the refrigerator and reheat it in a saucepan.

Prep: 25 minutes
Cook: 5 to 6 hours (low) or 2½ to 3 hours (high)
Makes: 28 (¼-cup) servings

- 1 **pound bulk Italian sausage**
- ⅓ **cup chopped onion**
- 4 **cloves garlic, minced**
- 2 **15-ounce cans tomato sauce**
- 1 **14.5-ounce can tomatoes, undrained, cut up**
- 1 **6-ounce can tomato paste**
- 4 **teaspoons dried oregano, crushed**
- 1 **tablespoon dried basil, crushed**
- 2 **teaspoons sugar**
- ¼ **teaspoon cayenne pepper**
- ½ **cup chopped pitted ripe olives**

   Assorted dippers (such as toasted bread slices sprinkled with Parmesan cheese, breadsticks, breaded mozzarella cheese sticks, and/or sweet pepper strips)

1 In a large skillet, cook sausage, onion, and garlic until meat is brown and onion is tender. Drain off fat.

2 In a 3½- or 4-quart slow cooker, combine sausage mixture, tomato sauce, undrained tomatoes, tomato paste, oregano, basil, sugar, and cayenne pepper.

3 Cover and cook on low-heat setting for 5 to 6 hours or on high-heat setting for 2½ to 3 hours.

4 Stir in olives. Serve with assorted dippers.

Nutrition facts per serving (dip only): 70 cal., 4 g total fat (2 g sat. fat), 11 mg chol., 275 mg sodium, 4 g carbo., 1 g fiber, 3 g pro.

pizza BY THE YARD

If you like, sprinkle on some sliced olives for more flavor.

Prep: 20 minutes
Cook: 5 to 6 hours (low) or 2½ to
      3 hours (high)
Makes: 20 to 24 servings

- **2 pounds bulk Italian sausage**
- **1 26-ounce jar garlic and mushroom pasta sauce**
- **2 large green and/or red sweet peppers, chopped**
- **1 1-pound loaf Italian bread, split lengthwise and toasted***
- **1 8-ounce package shredded pizza cheese (2 cups)**

1 In a large skillet, cook sausage over medium heat until brown. Drain off fat. In a 3½- or 4-quart slow cooker, combine sausage, pasta sauce, and sweet peppers.

2 Cover and cook on low-heat setting for 5 to 6 hours or on high-heat setting for 2½ to 3 hours.

3 Spoon sausage mixture over toasted bread. Sprinkle with cheese.

***Note:** To toast bread, preheat broiler. Place bread, cut sides up, on a baking sheet. Broil 3 to 4 inches from heat for 3 to 4 minutes or until toasted.

Nutrition facts per serving: 264 cal., 14 g total fat (6 g sat. fat), 39 mg chol., 608 mg sodium, 18 g carbo., 1 g fiber, 12 g pro.

georgia PEACH RIBS

Peach preserves from a jar make this an easy sauce. A touch of bourbon rounds out the wonderful flavor.

Prep: 15 minutes
Cook: 5 to 6 hours (low) or 2½ to
3 hours (high)
Makes: 12 servings

2½ **pounds pork loin back ribs***

1 **12-ounce jar peach preserves**

½ **cup finely chopped onion
(1 medium)**

1 **tablespoon bourbon**

1 **tablespoon yellow mustard**

1 **tablespoon cider vinegar**

¼ **teaspoon salt**

¼ **teaspoon cayenne pepper**

1 Cut ribs into single-rib portions. Place ribs in a 3½- or 4-quart slow cooker. In a medium bowl, combine peach preserves, onion, bourbon, mustard, vinegar, salt, and cayenne pepper. Pour over ribs, tossing to coat.

2 Cover and cook on low-heat setting for 5 to 6 hours or on high-heat setting for 2½ to 3 hours. Serve immediately or keep covered on warm or low-heat setting for up to 2 hours. Use tongs to remove ribs from cooking liquid to serve.

*Test Kitchen Tip: To make eating the ribs easier, have your butcher saw the ribs in half crosswise (across the bone) for smaller rib portions.

Nutrition facts per serving: 205 cal., 13 g total fat (5 g sat. fat), 47 mg chol., 80 mg sodium, 10 g carbo., 0 g fiber, 10 g pro.

flamin' CAJUN RIBLETS

To make the ribs easier to eat, ask your butcher to cut the ribs in half crosswise (across the bones) to make smaller portions.

Prep: 20 minutes
Cook: 5 to 6 hours (low) or 2½ to 3 hours (high)
Makes: 12 servings

- 3 **pounds pork loin back ribs**
- 1 **tablespoon Cajun seasoning**
- 1 **cup bottled chili sauce**
- 1 **medium onion, finely chopped**
- 1 **serrano chile pepper, seeded and finely chopped***
- 2 **tablespoons quick-cooking tapioca, crushed**
- 1 **teaspoon finely shredded lemon peel**
- 1 **tablespoon lemon juice**
- 1 **to 2 teaspoons bottled hot pepper sauce**
- **Snipped fresh parsley (optional)**

1 Sprinkle ribs with Cajun seasoning and rub in with your fingers. Cut ribs into single-rib portions. Place ribs in a 3½- or 4-quart slow cooker.

2 In a medium bowl, combine chili sauce, onion, serrano pepper, tapioca, lemon peel, lemon juice, and hot pepper sauce. Pour over ribs.

3 Cover and cook on low-heat setting for 5 to 6 hours or on high-heat setting for 2½ to 3 hours. Serve immediately or keep covered on warm or low-heat setting for up to 2 hours. (Remove any bones without meat.) If desired, sprinkle with parsley.

*Test Kitchen Tip: Because chile peppers, such as jalapeños, contain volatile oils that can burn your skin and eyes, avoid direct contact with chiles as much as possible. When working with chile peppers, wear plastic or rubber gloves. If your bare hands do touch the chile peppers, wash your hands well with soap and water.

Nutrition facts per serving: 231 cal., 17 g total fat (6 g sat. fat), 57 mg chol., 369 mg sodium, 7 g carbo., 1 g fiber, 12 g pro.

buffalo WINGS WITH BLUE CHEESE DIP

Just two ingredients take chicken wings from ho-hum to yum. If time permits, make the homemade dip. It will make the wings even more appetizing.

Prep: 35 minutes
Broil: 12 minutes
Cook: 4 to 5 hours (low) or 2 to
2½ hours (high)
Makes: 32 servings

- 16 chicken wings (about
3 pounds)
- 1¼ cups bottled chili sauce
- 2 tablespoons bottled hot
pepper sauce
- Blue Cheese Dip* or bottled
ranch salad dressing

1 Cut off and discard tips of chicken wings. Cut wings at joints to form 32 pieces. Place chicken pieces on the unheated rack of a broiler pan. Broil 3 to 4 inches from the heat for about 12 minutes or until light brown, turning once. Place chicken pieces in a 3½- or 4-quart slow cooker.

2 In a small bowl, combine chili sauce and hot pepper sauce. Pour over chicken.

3 Cover and cook on low-heat setting for 4 to 5 hours or on high-heat setting for 2 to 2½ hours. Serve chicken wings with Blue Cheese Dip.

*Blue Cheese Dip: In a blender, combine one 8-ounce carton dairy sour cream; ½ cup mayonnaise or salad dressing; ½ cup (2 ounces) crumbled blue cheese; 1 clove garlic, minced; and 1 tablespoon white wine vinegar or white vinegar. Cover and blend until smooth. Cover and chill for up to 1 week. If desired, top with additional crumbled blue cheese before serving.

Nutrition facts per serving: 108 cal., 8 g total fat (3 g sat. fat), 21 mg chol., 217 mg sodium, 3 g carbo., 0 g fiber, 6 g pro.

five-spice CHICKEN WINGS

Five-spice powder is often found in Asian-inspired dishes such as these tangy appetizer wings. The spice incorporates the five basic flavors of Chinese cooking: sweet, sour, bitter, savory, and salty.

Prep: 20 minutes
Bake: 20 minutes
Cook: 4 to 5 hours (low) or 2 to
     2½ hours (high)
Makes: 16 servings

  3 **pounds chicken wings
     (about 16)**

  1 **cup bottled plum sauce**

  2 **tablespoons butter, melted**

1½ **teaspoon five-spice powder**

    **Thin orange wedges and
    pineapple slices (optional)**

1 If desired, use a sharp knife to carefully cut off tips of the wings; discard wing tips. In a foil-lined 15×10×1-inch shallow baking pan, arrange wing pieces in a single layer. Bake in a 375°F oven for 20 minutes. Drain well.

2 For sauce, in a 3½- or 4-quart slow cooker combine plum sauce, melted butter, and five-spice powder. Add wing pieces, stirring to coat with sauce.

3 Cover and cook on low-heat setting for 4 to 5 hours or on high-heat setting for 2 to 2½ hours.

4 Serve immediately or keep covered on low-heat setting for up to 2 hours. If desired, garnish with orange wedges and pineapple slices.

Kentucky Chicken Wings: Prepare chicken as in Step 1. For sauce, in slow cooker combine ½ cup maple syrup, ½ cup whiskey, and 2 tablespoons melted butter. Add wing pieces, stirring to coat with sauce. Continue as in Step 3.

Buffalo-Style Chicken Wings: Prepare chicken as in Step 1. For sauce, in slow cooker combine 1½ cups hot-style barbecue sauce, 2 tablespoons melted butter, and 1 to 2 teaspoons bottled hot pepper sauce. Add wing pieces, stirring to coat with sauce. Continue as in Step 3. Serve with bottled blue cheese or ranch salad dressing. Omit the fruit garnish.

Nutrition facts per serving: 88 cal., 6 g total fat (2 g sat. fat), 35 mg chol., 41 mg sodium, 3 g carbo., 0 g fiber, 6 g pro.

sweet, HOT, AND SOUR MEATBALLS

To make uniform-size meatballs, pat the meat mixture into a 6-inch square and cut into 36 pieces. Shape each piece into a ball.

Prep: 35 minutes
Bake: 25 minutes
Cook: 3 to 4 hours (low) or 1½ to 2 hours (high)
Makes: 36 meatballs

 2 **eggs**

½ **cup fine dry bread crumbs**

½ **cup finely chopped onion (1 medium)**

¼ **cup milk**

½ **teaspoon salt**

½ **teaspoon ground black pepper**

 1 **pound bulk pork sausage**

 1 **pound ground beef**

¾ **cup apple jelly**

⅓ **cup spicy brown mustard**

⅓ **cup whiskey or apple juice**

1½ **teaspoons Worcestershire sauce**

Dash bottled hot pepper sauce

1 Preheat oven to 375°F. In a large bowl, beat eggs with a fork. Stir in bread crumbs, onion, milk, salt, and pepper. Add sausage and beef; mix well. Shape into 36 meatballs. Place in a shallow baking pan. Bake for 25 to 30 minutes or until meatballs are cooked through (160°F). Drain off fat.

2 Place meatballs in a 3½- or 4-quart slow cooker. In a small bowl, stir together jelly, mustard, whiskey, Worcestershire sauce, and hot pepper sauce. Pour over meatballs.

3 Cover and cook on low-heat setting for 3 to 4 hours or on high-heat setting for 1½ to 2 hours. Serve immediately or keep covered on warm or low-heat setting for up to 2 hours.

Nutrition facts per meatball: 112 cal., 7 g total fat (3 g sat. fat), 28 mg chol., 195 mg sodium, 6 g carbo., 0 g fiber, 5 g pro.

meatball SLIDERS

Sliders are small bites of flavor in a bun. Here meatballs are smothered in a classic Italian marinara sauce. Don't forget the provolone cheese.

Prep: 10 minutes
Cook: 4 to 5 hours (low) or 2 to 2½ hours (high)
Makes: 24 appetizers

- 1 **large red onion, cut into thin wedges (1½ cups)**
- 2 **12-ounce packages frozen cooked Italian meatballs (24)**
- 1 **24- to 26-ounce jar marinara or pasta sauce (about 2¼ cups)**
- 1 **tablespoon balsamic vinegar**
- ½ **teaspoon crushed red pepper**
- 6 **slices provolone cheese, quartered (6 ounces)**
- 4 **roma tomatoes, sliced**
- 24 **cocktail buns, split and toasted, if desired**

1 Place onion wedges in a 3½- or 4-quart slow cooker. Top with meatballs. In a medium bowl, combine marinara sauce, balsamic vinegar, and crushed red pepper. Pour over meatballs.

2 Cover and cook on low-heat setting for 4 to 5 hours or on high-heat setting for 2 to 2½ hours.

3 Gently stir through mixture in cooker. Place a slice of provolone cheese and a slice of tomato on each cocktail bun bottom. Top each with a meatball and bun tops.

Nutrition facts per serving: 217 cal., 11 g total fat (5 g sat. fat), 24 mg chol., 516 mg sodium, 20 g carbo., 2 g fiber, 10 g pro.

apricot-glazed HAM BALLS

Here's a slick trick for uniformly shaped meatballs: Pat the meat mixture into a 6×5-inch rectangle on a piece of waxed paper. Cut the meat into 1-inch cubes, then use your hands to roll each cube into a ball.

Prep: 20 minutes
Bake: 20 minutes
Cook: 4 to 5 hours (low) or 1½ to 2 hours (high)
Makes: 30 meatballs

- 1 **egg, beaten**
- ½ **cup graham cracker crumbs**
- 2 **tablespoons unsweetened pineapple juice**
- 1 **teaspoon dry mustard**
- ¼ **teaspoon salt**
- ½ **pound ground fully cooked ham**
- ½ **pound ground pork**
- ½ **cup snipped dried apricots**
- 1 **18-ounce jar apricot preserves**
- ⅓ **cup unsweetened pineapple juice**
- 1 **tablespoon cider vinegar**
- ½ **teaspoon ground ginger**

1 For meatballs, in a large bowl combine egg, graham cracker crumbs, the 2 tablespoons pineapple juice, dry mustard, and salt. Add ground ham, ground pork, and snipped apricots; mix well. Shape into 30 meatballs. In a 15×10×1-inch baking pan, arrange meatballs in a single layer. Bake, uncovered, in a 350°F oven for 20 minutes. Drain well. In a 3½- or 4-quart slow cooker, place cooked meatballs.

2 For sauce, in a small bowl combine apricot preserves, the ⅓ cup pineapple juice, vinegar, and ginger. Pour sauce over meatballs.

3 Cover and cook on low-heat setting for 4 to 5 hours or on high-heat setting for 1½ to 2 hours.

4 Serve immediately or keep covered on low-heat setting for up to 2 hours. Gently stir just before serving. Serve with toothpicks.

Nutrition facts per serving: 86 cal., 2 g total fat (1 g sat. fat), 15 mg chol., 151 mg sodium, 15 g carbo., 0 g fiber, 3 g pro.

plum-good SAUSAGE AND MEATBALLS

Although this recipe calls for a package of 16 meatballs, various brands contain different counts. Just look for the total weight, even if it isn't a 16 count.

Prep: 10 minutes
Cook: 5 to 6 hours (low) or 2½ to 3 hours (high)
Makes: 16 servings

- 1 **10- or 12-ounce jar plum jam or preserves**
- 1 **18-ounce bottle barbecue sauce**
- 1 **16-ounce link cooked jalapeño pepper smoked sausage or smoked sausage, sliced into bite-size pieces**
- 1 **16- to 18-ounce package Italian-style or regular frozen cooked meatballs, thawed**

1 In a 3½- or 4-quart slow cooker, combine jam, barbecue sauce, sausage, and meatballs.

2 Cover and cook on low-heat setting for 5 to 6 hours or on high-heat setting for 2½ to 3 hours.

3 Serve immediately or keep covered on warm or low-heat setting for up to 2 hours. Stir occasionally.

Nutrition facts per serving: 267 cal., 16 g total fat (6 g sat. fat), 38 mg chol., 898 mg sodium, 19 g carbo., 2 g fiber, 12 g pro.

crock OF REUBENS

If your favorite bakery doesn't routinely carry mini buns, ask them to make some for you.

Prep: 20 minutes
Cook: 4 to 6 hours (low) or 2 to 3 hours (high)
Makes: 24 sandwiches

1 **2- to 3-pound corned beef brisket with spice packet**

1 **16-ounce jar sauerkraut, drained**

½ **cup bottled Thousand Island salad dressing**

24 **small rye or whole wheat rolls, split and toasted**

2 **cups shredded Swiss cheese (8 ounces)**

Bottled Thousand Island salad dressing (optional)

1 Trim fat from meat. If necessary, cut meat to fit into a 3½- or 4-quart slow cooker. Place meat in cooker. Sprinkle with spices from packet. Spread sauerkraut over the meat. Drizzle the ½ cup salad dressing over all.

2 Cover and cook on low-heat setting for 4 to 6 hours or on high-heat setting for 2 to 3 hours.

3 Remove meat from cooker and place on cutting board. Thinly slice meat against the grain. Return sliced meat to the cooker; stir to combine with the cooking liquid.

4 Using a slotted spoon, spoon corned beef mixture onto toasted rolls. Top with cheese and, if desired, additional salad dressing. If desired, secure with cocktail picks.

Nutrition facts per sandwich: 231 cal., 13 g total fat (5 g sat. fat), 47 mg chol., 1,165 mg sodium, 17 g carbo., 3 g fiber, 12 g pro.

savory
MEATS AND POULTRY

Country Captain, *recipe page 104*

boeuf À LA BOURGUIGNONNE

This classic French dish consists of fork-tender beef and a rich, seasoned wine gravy. It's a dish that never loses its crowd appeal.

Prep: 45 minutes
Cook: 10 to 12 hours (low) or
      5 to 6 hours (high)
Makes: 6 servings

  3 **slices bacon, coarsely chopped**
  2 **pounds boneless beef chuck roast**
1½ **cups chopped onions (3 medium)**
  2 **cloves garlic, minced**
  4 **stems fresh parsley**
  3 **sprigs fresh thyme**
  1 **sprig fresh rosemary**
  2 **bay leaves**
 ¼ **teaspoon whole black peppercorns**
  4 **medium carrots, cut into ¾-inch pieces**
  2 **cups frozen small whole onions**
  3 **tablespoons quick-cooking tapioca, crushed**
  1 **cup Burgundy**
 ½ **cup beef broth**
 ¼ **cup brandy**
  1 **tablespoon tomato paste**
  1 **tablespoon olive oil**
  1 **cup quartered fresh cremini mushrooms**
    Mashed potatoes
    Snipped fresh parsley

1 In a large skillet, cook bacon until crisp. Drain on paper towels. Reserve bacon drippings in skillet. Cover and chill cooked bacon until serving time. Trim fat from meat. Cut meat into 1-inch cubes. Heat bacon drippings over medium heat. Cook half of the meat in hot drippings until browned; remove from skillet. Add remaining meat, chopped onions, and garlic to skillet. Cook until meat is brown and onions are tender. Remove from heat; combine all meat in skillet.

2 For a spice bag, cut an 8-inch square from a double thickness of 100-percent-cotton cheesecloth. Place parsley, thyme, rosemary, bay leaves, and peppercorns in the center of the cheesecloth square. Bring up corners of the cheesecloth; tie closed with clean 100-percent-cotton kitchen string. Set aside.

3 In a 3½- or 4-quart slow cooker, combine carrots and whole onions. Sprinkle with tapioca. Spoon meat mixture over mixture in cooker. Add spice bag. In a small bowl, whisk together wine, broth, brandy, and tomato paste. Pour over mixture in cooker.

4 Cover and cook on low-heat setting for 10 to 12 hours or on high-heat setting for 5 to 6 hours. Remove spice bag and discard.

5 In a large skillet, heat oil over medium-high heat. Cook mushrooms in hot oil until brown. Serve beef with mashed potatoes. Top each serving with mushrooms, bacon, and snipped parsley.

Nutrition facts per serving: 616 cal., 30 g total fat (12 g sat. fat), 127 mg chol., 556 mg sodium, 37 g carbo., 5 g fiber, 36 g pro.

russian BRAISED BRISKET

Adding cabbage, mushrooms, and sauce just before the meat is finished cooking ensures that each part of the meal is just the right doneness at serving time.

Prep: 20 minutes
Cook: 10 hours (low) or 5 hours
(high) + 30 to 60 minutes
Makes: 6 servings

- 1 **2- to 3-pound beef brisket**
  Salt
  Ground black pepper
- 1 **tablespoon vegetable oil**
- 1 **large onion, cut into wedges**
- 2 **medium parsnips, cut into 2-inch pieces**
- 2 **medium carrots, cut into 2-inch pieces**
- ½ **teaspoon dill seeds**
- ½ **teaspoon caraway seeds**
- ¼ **teaspoon salt**
- 1½ **cups beef broth**
- ¼ **cup vodka (optional)**
- 1 **8-ounce carton dairy sour cream**
- ⅓ **cup all-purpose flour**
- ¼ **cup water**
- 2 **teaspoons dried dill**
- 2 **teaspoons horseradish mustard**
- 2 **cups finely shredded cabbage**
- 1 **cup sliced fresh mushrooms**

1 Trim fat from meat. Cut meat to fit into a 3½- or 4-quart slow cooker. Sprinkle meat with salt and pepper. In a large skillet, heat oil over medium-high heat. Cook meat on all sides in hot oil until brown.

2 In the slow cooker, combine onion, parsnips, and carrots. Sprinkle with dill seeds, caraway seeds, and ¼ teaspoon salt. Top with meat. Pour broth and vodka, if desired, over mixture in cooker.

3 Cover and cook on low-heat setting for 10 hours or on high-heat setting for 5 hours.

4 If using low-heat setting, turn to high-heat setting. In a medium bowl, stir together sour cream, flour, the water, dill, and mustard until smooth. Stir about 1 cup of the hot cooking liquid into the sour cream mixture. Add to cooker, stirring to combine. Stir in cabbage and mushrooms. Cover and cook for 30 to 60 minutes more or until vegetables are tender and liquid is thickened and bubbly.

5 Transfer meat to a serving platter; slice thinly across the grain. Using a slotted spoon, transfer vegetables to platter. Serve cooking liquid with meat and vegetables.

Nutrition facts per serving: 379 cal., 17 g total fat (7 g sat. fat), 79 mg chol., 589 mg sodium, 20 g carbo., 4 g fiber, 37 g pro.

smoky BARBECUED BEEF BRISKET

If you like, pile this zesty beef into buns or hard rolls and spoon on some creamy coleslaw as a topper.

Prep: 15 minutes
Cook: 10 to 11 hours (low) or
5 to 5½ hours (high)
Makes: 6 to 8 servings

- 1 2- to 3-pound fresh beef brisket
- 1 teaspoon chili powder
- ½ teaspoon garlic powder
- ¼ teaspoon celery seeds
- ⅛ teaspoon ground black pepper
- ½ cup ketchup
- ½ cup chili sauce
- ¼ cup packed brown sugar
- 2 tablespoons vinegar
- 2 tablespoons Worcestershire sauce
- 1½ teaspoons liquid smoke
- ½ teaspoon dry mustard
- ⅓ cup cold water
- 3 tablespoons all-purpose flour

1 Trim fat from meat. Cut meat to fit into a 3½- or 4-quart slow cooker. In a small bowl, combine chili powder, garlic powder, celery seeds, and pepper. Sprinkle chili powder mixture evenly over meat; rub in with your fingers. Place meat in the slow cooker.

2 In a medium bowl, combine ketchup, chili sauce, brown sugar, vinegar, Worcestershire sauce, liquid smoke, and dry mustard. Pour over meat in cooker.

3 Cover and cook on low-heat setting for 10 to 11 hours or on high-heat setting for 5 to 5½ hours.

4 Remove meat from cooker, reserving cooking juices. Skim fat off cooking juices; measure 2½ cups of the cooking juices. For sauce, in a medium saucepan, stir the cold water into flour; add the 2½ cups cooking juices. Cook and stir until thickened and bubbly; cook and stir for 1 minute more. Cutting across the grain, cut the meat into thin slices. Serve sauce with meat.

Nutrition facts per serving: 305 cal., 8 g total fat (2 g sat. fat), 87 mg chol., 681 mg sodium, 24 g carbo., 2 g fiber, 34 g pro.

country ITALIAN BEEF

Fennel and basil are an appealing change of pace in this bold-flavored beef stew.

Prep: 25 minutes
Cook: 8 to 10 hours (low) or
      4 to 5 hours (high)
Makes: 6 to 8 servings

- 2 **pounds boneless beef chuck**
- 8 **ounces tiny new potatoes, halved or quartered**
- 2 **medium carrots or parsnips, peeled and cut into 1- to 2-inch pieces**
- 1 **cup chopped onion**
- 1 **medium fennel bulb, trimmed and cut into ½-inch-thick wedges**
- 1 **14-ounce can beef broth**
- 1 **cup dry red wine or beef broth**
- 1 **6-ounce can tomato paste**
- 2 **tablespoons quick-cooking tapioca**
- 1 **teaspoon dried rosemary, crushed**
- ½ **teaspoon ground black pepper**
- 4 **cloves garlic, minced**
- 1 **to 2 cups fresh basil leaves, fresh spinach leaves, or torn fresh escarole**

1 Trim fat from meat. Cut meat into 2-inch pieces. Set aside.

2 In a 4- to 5-quart slow cooker, combine potatoes, carrots, onion, and fennel. Add meat.

3 In a medium bowl, combine broth, wine, tomato paste, tapioca, rosemary, pepper, and garlic. Pour over mixture in cooker.

4 Cover and cook on low-heat setting for 8 to 10 hours or on high-heat setting for 4 to 5 hours. Just before serving, stir in basil.

Nutrition facts per serving: 319 cal., 6 g total fat (2 g sat. fat), 89 mg chol., 596 mg sodium, 23 g carbo., 4 g fiber, 36 g pro.

beef GOULASH

Depending on how much heat you like, choose sweet or hot Hungarian paprika to spice this goulash.

Prep: 25 minutes
Cook: 8 to 9 hours (low) or
3½ to 4½ hours (high),
+ 30 minutes on high
Makes: 6 servings

1½ pounds beef stew meat

2 medium carrots, bias-cut into
½-inch-thick slices

2 medium onions, thinly sliced

3 cloves garlic, minced

1¼ cups beef broth

1 6-ounce can tomato paste

1 tablespoon Hungarian
paprika

1 teaspoon finely shredded
lemon peel

½ teaspoon salt

½ teaspoon caraway seeds

¼ teaspoon ground black pepper

1 bay leaf

1 red or green sweet pepper,
cut into bite-size strips

Hot cooked noodles

Dairy sour cream or yogurt

Hungarian paprika (optional)

1 In a 3½- or 4-quart slow cooker, combine meat, carrots, onions, and garlic. In a small bowl, combine broth, tomato paste, the 1 tablespoon paprika, the lemon peel, salt, caraway seeds, black pepper, and bay leaf. Stir into vegetable and meat mixture in cooker.

2 Cover and cook on low-heat setting for 8 to 9 hours or on high-heat setting for 3½ to 4½ hours.

3 If using low-heat setting, turn to high-heat setting. Stir in sweet pepper. Cover and cook for 30 minutes more. Discard bay leaf. Serve with noodles. Top with sour cream. If desired, sprinkle with additional paprika.

Nutrition facts per serving: 356 cal., 11 g total fat (4 g sat. fat), 85 mg chol., 678 mg sodium, 33 g carbo., 4 g fiber, 32 g pro.

german-style BEEF ROAST

Red wine, chopped dill pickles, and hearty mustard set this succulent beef pot roast apart from the rest.

Prep: 25 minutes
Cook: 8 to 10 hours (low) or
4 to 5 hours (high)
Makes: 8 servings

- 1 2½- to 3-pound boneless beef chuck pot roast
- 1 tablespoon cooking oil
- 2 cups sliced carrot
- 2 cups chopped onion
- 1 cup sliced celery
- ¾ cup chopped kosher-style dill pickles
- ½ cup dry red wine or beef broth
- ⅓ cup German-style mustard
- ½ teaspoon coarsely ground black pepper
- ¼ teaspoon ground cloves
- 2 bay leaves
- 2 tablespoons all-purpose flour
- 2 tablespoons dry red wine or beef broth
- Hot cooked spaetzle or cooked noodles
- Snipped fresh parsley (optional)

1 Trim fat from meat. If necessary, cut meat to fit in a 3½- or 4-quart slow cooker. In a large skillet, brown the meat slowly on all sides in hot oil.

2 In the cooker, combine carrot, onion, celery, and pickles. Place the meat on top of the vegetables. In a small bowl, combine the ½ cup red wine, the mustard, pepper, cloves, and bay leaves. Pour over meat and vegetables in cooker.

3 Cover and cook on low-heat setting for 8 to 10 hours or on high-heat setting for 4 to 5 hours.

4 Transfer meat to serving platter; cover to keep warm. For gravy: Transfer vegetables and cooking liquid to a 2-quart saucepan. Skim off fat. Discard bay leaves. In a small bowl, stir together flour and the 2 tablespoons red wine. Stir into mixture in saucepan. Cook and stir over medium heat until thickened and bubbly. Cook and stir for 1 minute more. Slice meat. Serve with vegetables, gravy, and hot cooked spaetzle. If desired, sprinkle with parsley.

Nutrition facts per serving: 372 cal., 25 g total fat (9 g sat. fat), 82 mg chol., 414 mg sodium, 10 g carbo., 2 g fiber, 24 g pro.

polenta WITH GROUND BEEF RAGOÛT

Ground pork or lamb would be equally tasty in this hearty stew.

Prep: 25 minutes
Cook: 7 to 9 hours (low) or
       3½ to 4½ hours (high),
       + 30 minutes on high
Makes: 6 servings

- 1 **pound lean ground beef**
- 1 **14.5-ounce can Italian-style stewed tomatoes, undrained**
- 3 **medium carrots, cut into ½-inch-thick slices**
- 2 **medium onions, cut into thin wedges**
- 1 **large red sweet pepper, cut into 1-inch pieces**
- ½ **cup beef broth**
- ¼ **teaspoon salt**
- ¼ **teaspoon ground black pepper**
- 6 **cloves garlic, minced**
- 1 **medium zucchini, halved lengthwise and cut into ¼-inch-thick slices**
- 1 **16-ounce tube refrigerated cooked polenta**
- 6 **tablespoons purchased pesto or olive tapenade**
- **Fresh basil sprigs (optional)**

1 In a large skillet, cook meat until brown. Drain off fat. Transfer meat to a 3½- or 4-quart slow cooker. Stir in undrained tomatoes, carrots, onions, sweet pepper, broth, salt, black pepper, and garlic.

2 Cover and cook on low-heat setting for 7 to 9 hours or on high-heat setting for 3½ to 4½ hours.

3 If using low-heat setting, turn to high-heat setting. Stir in zucchini. Cover and cook for about 30 minutes more or until zucchini is crisp-tender.

4 Meanwhile, prepare polenta according to package directions. Serve meat mixture over polenta. Top individual servings with pesto. If desired, garnish with basil sprigs.

Nutrition facts per serving: 388 cal., 20 g total fat (4 g sat. fat), 50 mg chol., 773 mg sodium, 30 g carbo., 5 g fiber, 20 g pro.

jerk BEEF ROAST

Jamaican jerk seasoning is the must-have ingredient for this roast. You'll enjoy its spicy-sweet combination of chiles, thyme, cinnamon, ginger, allspice, and cloves.

Prep: 30 minutes
Cook: 8 to 10 hours (low) or
　　　 4 to 5 hours (high)
Makes: 6 servings

- **1 2- to 2½-pound boneless beef chuck pot roast**
- **¾ cup water**
- **¼ cup raisins**
- **¼ cup steak sauce**
- **3 tablespoons balsamic vinegar**
- **2 tablespoons sugar (optional)**
- **2 tablespoons quick-cooking tapioca**
- **1 teaspoon cracked black pepper**
- **1 teaspoon Jamaican jerk seasoning**
- **2 cloves garlic, minced**
- **Hot cooked brown rice (optional)**

1 Trim fat from meat. If necessary, cut roast to fit into a 3½- or 4-quart slow cooker. Place meat in the cooker. In a medium bowl, combine the water, raisins, steak sauce, balsamic vinegar, sugar (if desired), tapioca, pepper, Jamaican jerk seasoning, and garlic. Pour mixture over roast.

2 Cover and cook on low-heat setting for 8 to 10 hours or on high-heat setting for 4 to 5 hours. Skim fat from the cooking liquid. Serve beef with the cooking liquid and, if desired, hot cooked rice.

Nutrition facts per serving: 237 cal., 6 g total fat (2 g sat. fat), 89 mg chol., 310 mg sodium, 12 g carbo., 1 g fiber, 33 g pro.

saucy POT ROAST WITH NOODLES

Prep: 25 minutes
Cook: 10 to 12 hours (low) or
    4 to 5 hours (high)
Makes: 6 to 8 servings

- 1 **2- to 2½-pound beef chuck pot roast**
- 1 **tablespoon cooking oil**
- 2 **medium carrots, sliced**
- 2 **stalks celery, sliced**
- 1 **medium onion, sliced**
- 2 **cloves garlic, minced**
- 1 **tablespoon quick-cooking tapioca**
- 1 **14.5-ounce can Italian-style stewed tomatoes, undrained**
- 1 **6-ounce can Italian-style tomato paste**
- 1 **tablespoon packed brown sugar**
- ½ **teaspoon salt**
- ¼ **teaspoon ground black pepper**
- 1 **bay leaf**
  Hot cooked noodles
  Celery leaves (optional)

1 Trim fat from meat. If necessary, cut meat to fit into a 3½- or 4-quart slow cooker. In a large skillet, brown meat on all sides in hot oil.

2 In the cooker, combine carrots, celery, onion, and garlic. Sprinkle tapioca over vegetables. Arrange meat to cover vegetables.

3 In a medium bowl, combine undrained tomatoes, tomato paste, brown sugar, salt, pepper, and bay leaf; pour over the roast in cooker.

4 Cover and cook on low-heat setting for 10 to 12 hours or on high-setting for 4 to 5 hours.

5 Discard bay leaf. Skim off fat. Slice meat. Serve with noodles. If desired, garnish with celery leaves.

Nutrition facts per serving: 569 cal., 27 g total fat (10 g sat. fat), 127 mg chol., 693 mg sodium, 48 g carbo., 4 g fiber, 32 g pro.

dijon PEPPER STEAK

Pepper steak is a classic dish that starts with pressing cracked black pepper into the meat and finishes with an easily made sauce. This slow-cooker version sticks to those basics.

Prep: 20 minutes
Cook: 8 to 10 hours (low) or
      4 to 5 hours (high)
Makes: 6 servings

- 2 **pounds boneless beef sirloin steak, cut 1 inch thick**
- 1½ **teaspoons cracked black pepper**
- 1 **tablespoon cooking oil**
- 2 **cups packaged peeled baby carrots**
- 1 **medium onion, sliced**
- 1 **10.75-ounce can condensed cream of celery soup**
- ¼ **cup Dijon-style mustard**
- **Hot cooked noodles or hot mashed potatoes (optional)**

① Trim fat from meat. Cut meat into 6 serving-size pieces. Sprinkle cracked black pepper evenly over meat; press in with your fingers. In a large skillet, brown meat, half at a time, in hot oil. Drain off fat. Set aside.

② In a 3½- to 4½-quart slow cooker, combine carrots and onion. Add meat. In a medium bowl, stir together cream of celery soup and Dijon mustard. Pour over mixture in cooker.

③ Cover and cook on low-heat setting for 8 to 10 hours or on high-heat setting for 4 to 5 hours. If desired, serve over hot cooked noodles.

Nutrition facts per serving: 266 cal., 9 g total fat (2 g sat. fat), 96 mg chol., 716 mg sodium, 9 g carbo., 2 g fiber, 33 g pro.

mexican-stuffed SWEET PEPPERS

The colorful sweet peppers are perfect containers for the zesty filling of ground meat, cheese, and salsa.

Prep: 25 minutes
Cook: 6 to 7 hours (low) or
3 to 3½ hours (high)
Makes: 4 servings

- **4 medium green, red, and/or yellow sweet peppers**
- **1 pound lean ground beef or ground pork**
- **1 16-ounce jar black bean salsa or chunky salsa**
- **1½ cups Monterey Jack cheese with jalapeño chile peppers or Monterey Jack cheese, shredded (6 ounces)**
- **1 cup quick-cooking white rice**
- **1 cup water**

1 Remove tops, membranes, and seeds from sweet peppers. For filling, in a large skillet, cook meat until brown; drain off fat. Stir salsa, 1 cup of the cheese, and the uncooked rice into meat in skillet. Spoon filling into peppers, mounding as needed.

2 Pour the water into a 4½- or 5-quart slow cooker. Arrange peppers, filling up, in the cooker.

3 Cover and cook on low-heat setting for 6 to 7 hours or on high-heat setting for 3 to 3½ hours. Transfer peppers to a serving platter. Top with remaining cheese.

Nutrition facts per serving: 513 cal., 24 g total fat (12 g sat. fat), 109 mg chol., 1,060 mg sodium, 38 g carbo., 2 g fiber, 37 g pro.

beef FAJITAS

Prep: 25 minutes
Cook: 7 to 8 hours (low) or
     3½ to 4 hours (high)
Makes: 8 servings

- 1   **large onion, cut into thin wedges**
- 2   **pounds boneless beef sirloin steak**
- 1   **teaspoon ground cumin**
- 1   **teaspoon ground coriander**
- ½   **teaspoon salt**
- ½   **teaspoon ground black pepper**
- 2   **medium red or green sweet peppers, cut into thin, bite-size strips**
- ¼   **cup beef broth**
- 8   **7- to 8-inch whole wheat or plain flour tortillas**
- 1   **cup shredded carrot**
- 1   **cup coarsely shredded lettuce**
     Salsa, sour cream, and guacamole

1 Place onion in a 3½- or 4-quart slow cooker. Trim fat from meat. Sprinkle one side of the meat with cumin, coriander, salt, and black pepper; rub in with your fingers. Cut meat across the grain into thin, bite-size strips. Add meat strips to cooker. Top with sweet pepper. Pour broth over all.

2 Cover and cook on low-heat setting for 7 to 8 hours or on high-heat setting for 3½ to 4 hours.

3 To serve, use a slotted spoon to spoon meat-vegetable mixture onto tortillas. Top each serving with carrot and lettuce. Fold tortillas over. Serve with salsa, sour cream, and guacamole.

Nutrition facts per serving: 327 cal., 10 g total fat (3 g sat. fat), 70 mg chol., 642 mg sodium, 22 g carbo., 12 g fiber, 33 g pro.

italian BEEF SANDWICHES

Roasted red sweet peppers give these herbed beef sandwiches authentic flavor.

Prep: 15 minutes
Cook: 7 to 8 hours (low) or
          3½ to 4 hours (high)
Makes: 2 sandwiches

 6 **ounces beef flank steak**

 ½ **teaspoon dried oregano,
     crushed**

    Dash crushed red pepper

 1 **clove garlic, minced**

 ½ **cup low-sodium tomato juice**

 ¼ **cup bottled roasted red sweet
     pepper strips (optional)**

 2 **4-inch-long pieces French
     bread, split and toasted**

 ¼ **cup shredded provolone
     cheese (1 ounce)**

1 Trim fat from meat. If necessary, cut meat to fit into a 1½-quart slow cooker. Place meat in cooker. Sprinkle with oregano, crushed red pepper, and garlic. Pour tomato juice over all.

2 Cover and cook on low-heat setting for 7 to 8 hours or on high-heat setting for 3½ to 4 hours. If no heat setting is available, cook for 6 to 7 hours.

3 Remove meat from cooker, reserving cooking juices. Using two forks, shred the meat. If desired, stir roasted pepper strips into shredded meat. Place shredded meat on bottoms of French bread pieces. Drizzle enough of the cooking juices over meat to moisten. Sprinkle shredded meat with cheese. Cover with tops of French bread pieces.

Nutrition facts per serving: 302 cal., 11 g total fat (5 g sat. fat), 44 mg chol., 442 mg sodium, 23 g carbo., 2 g fiber, 26 g pro.

north AFRICAN BEEF STEW

Cumin, cayenne, and cinnamon give this beef-and-fruit stew its interesting North African flavor.

Prep: 20 minutes
Cook: 7½ to 8½ hours (low),
      + 30 minutes, or
      3½ to 4 hours (high),
      + 30 minutes
Makes: 6 servings

1½ **pounds lean beef stew meat**

2 **medium sweet potatoes, peeled, halved lengthwise, and cut into ½-inch-thick slices**

1 **medium onion, cut into wedges**

1 **cup water**

1 **teaspoon instant beef bouillon granules**

¾ **teaspoon ground cumin**

¼ **teaspoon cayenne pepper**

⅛ **teaspoon ground cinnamon**

4 **cloves garlic, minced**

1 **14.5-ounce can diced tomatoes, undrained**

½ **cup dried apricots or pitted dried plums (prunes), quartered**

  Hot cooked couscous (optional)

¼ **cup chopped peanuts**

1 Cut meat into 1-inch pieces. In a 3½- or 4-quart slow cooker, combine meat, sweet potatoes, and onion. Stir in the water, bouillon granules, cumin, cayenne pepper, cinnamon, and garlic.

2 Cover and cook on low-heat setting for 7½ to 8½ hours or on high-heat setting for 3½ to 4 hours.

3 Stir in undrained tomatoes and dried apricots. Cover and cook for 30 minutes more. If desired, serve meat mixture over hot cooked couscous. Sprinkle individual servings with peanuts.

Nutrition facts per serving: 274 cal., 7 g total fat (2 g sat. fat), 67 mg chol., 373 mg sodium, 24 g carbo., 4 g fiber, 27 g pro.

ginger-AND-ORANGE-GLAZED
SHORT RIBS

When it comes to a down-to-earth comfort meal, it's hard to beat beef short ribs. Here, the ribs get special treatment with five-spice powder and other Asian flavorings.

Prep: 20 minutes
Cook: 11 to 12 hours (low) or
5½ to 6 hours (high)
Makes: 4 to 6 servings

  3 **pounds beef short ribs**

  1 **large red onion, cut into wedges**

  1 **cup orange marmalade**

  ⅓ **cup water**

  2 **tablespoons rice vinegar**

  1 **tablespoon soy sauce**

  2 **teaspoons five-spice powder**

  2 **teaspoons grated fresh ginger**

  ½ **to 1½ teaspoons chile oil**

  2 **cloves garlic, minced**

1 Trim fat from short ribs. Place red onion in a 3½- to 5-quart slow cooker. Add short ribs. In a medium bowl, combine orange marmalade, the water, rice vinegar, soy sauce, five-spice powder, ginger, chile oil, and garlic. Reserve ⅔ cup of the marmalade mixture for sauce; cover and chill. Pour the remaining marmalade mixture over ribs and onion in cooker.

2 Cover and cook on low-heat setting for 11 to 12 hours or on high-heat setting for 5½ to 6 hours.

3 For sauce, in a small saucepan, heat reserved marmalade mixture until boiling; reduce heat. Boil gently, uncovered, for 5 minutes. Remove short ribs and onion from cooker; discard cooking liquid. Serve short ribs and onion with sauce.

Nutrition facts per serving: 452 cal., 12 g total fat (5 g sat. fat), 64 mg chol., 385 mg sodium, 58 g carbo., 1 g fiber, 29 g pro.

gingered BEEF AND VEGETABLES

Prep: 20 minutes
Cook: 9 to 10 hours (low) or
4½ to 5 hours (high),
+ 20 minutes on high
Makes: 6 servings

1½ pounds boneless beef round
steak, cut into 1-inch cubes

 4 medium carrots, bias-cut into
½-inch-thick slices

 ½ cup bias-sliced green onions

 2 cloves garlic, minced

1½ cups water

 2 tablespoons soy sauce

 2 teaspoons grated fresh
ginger

1½ teaspoons instant beef
bouillon granules

 ¼ teaspoon crushed red pepper

 3 tablespoons cornstarch

 3 tablespoons cold water

 ½ cup chopped red sweet
pepper

 2 cups loose-pack frozen sugar
snap peas, thawed

Hot cooked rice

1 In a 3½- or 4-quart slow cooker, combine meat, carrots, green onions, and garlic. In a medium bowl, combine the 1½ cups water, the soy sauce, ginger, bouillon granules, and crushed red pepper; pour over mixture in cooker.

2 Cover and cook on low-heat setting for 9 to 10 hours or on high-heat setting for 4½ to 5 hours.

3 If using low-heat setting, turn to high-heat setting. In a small bowl, stir together cornstarch and the 3 tablespoons cold water; stir into meat mixture along with sweet pepper. Cover and cook for 20 to 30 minutes or until thickened, stirring once. Stir in sugar snap peas. Serve with hot cooked rice.

Nutrition facts per serving: 350 cal., 10 g total fat (4 g sat. fat), 68 mg chol., 400 mg sodium, 35 g carbo., 3 g fiber, 29 g pro.

beef LO MEIN

Thanks to ready-made stir-fry sauce and your slow cooker, this Asian classic has never been easier!

Prep: 25 minutes
Cook: 7 to 9 hours (low) or
3½ to 4½ hours (high),
+ 30 minutes on high
Makes: 8 servings

- 2 **pounds boneless beef sirloin steak, cut 1 inch thick**
- 1 **tablespoon cooking oil**
- 1 **large onion, sliced**
- 1 **8-ounce can sliced water chestnuts, drained**
- 1 **4.5-ounce jar (drained weight) whole mushrooms, drained**
- 1 **12.1-ounce jar stir-fry sauce**
- 1 **tablespoon quick-cooking tapioca**
- 1 **16-ounce package loose-pack frozen broccoli, cauliflower, and carrots**
- ⅓ **cup cashews**
- 12 **ounces dried lo mein noodles**

1 Trim fat from meat. Cut meat into 1-inch pieces. In a large skillet, brown meat, half at a time, in hot oil. Drain off fat. Set aside.

2 Place onion in a 3½- or 4-quart slow cooker. Add meat, water chestnuts, and mushrooms. In a small bowl, stir together stir-fry sauce and tapioca. Pour over mixture in cooker.

3 Cover and cook on low-heat setting for 7 to 9 hours or on high-heat setting for 3½ to 4½ hours.

4 If using low-heat setting, turn to high-heat setting. Stir in frozen vegetables. Cover and cook for 30 to 40 minutes more or until vegetables are crisp-tender. Stir in cashews. Meanwhile, cook lo mein noodles according to package directions; drain. Serve meat mixture over lo mein noodles.

Nutrition facts per serving: 447 cal., 11 g total fat (2 g sat. fat), 95 mg chol., 995 mg sodium, 52 g carbo., 4 g fiber, 35 g pro.

moroccan-style SHORT RIBS

Couscous flecked with almonds and olives provides a soothing counterpoint to these spicy beef short ribs, garbanzo beans, and vegetables.

Prep: 30 minutes
Cook: 9 to 10 hours (low) or
4½ to 5 hours (high)
Makes: 8 servings

- 1 **tablespoon dried thyme, crushed**
- 1 **teaspoon salt**
- 1 **teaspoon ground ginger**
- 1 **teaspoon ground black pepper**
- ½ **teaspoon ground cinnamon**
- 3½ **pounds beef short ribs**
- 2 **tablespoons olive oil**
- 3 **cups beef broth**
- 1 **16-ounce can garbanzo beans (chickpeas), rinsed and drained**
- 1 **14.5-ounce can diced tomatoes, undrained**
- 1 **large onion, cut into thin wedges**
- 1 **medium fennel bulb, trimmed and cut into thin wedges**
- 1 **cup chopped carrot**
- 4 **cloves garlic, minced**
- 1 **10-ounce package quick-cooking couscous**
- ½ **cup sliced almonds, toasted**
- ½ **cup pitted kalamata olives, halved**

1 In a small bowl, combine thyme, salt, ginger, pepper, and cinnamon. Sprinkle evenly over short ribs; rub in with your fingers. In a large skillet, brown short ribs, half at a time, in hot oil over medium-high heat. Drain off fat. In a 6- to 7-quart slow cooker, combine broth, beans, undrained tomatoes, onion, fennel, carrot, and garlic; top with short ribs.

2 Cover and cook on low-heat setting for 9 to 10 hours or on high-heat setting for 4½ to 5 hours. Using a slotted spoon, transfer ribs and vegetables to a serving dish. If desired, moisten with cooking liquid. Meanwhile, prepare couscous according to package directions. Stir in almonds and olives. Serve with short ribs and vegetables.

Nutrition facts per serving: 441 cal., 17 g total fat (4 g sat. fat), 46 mg chol., 1,064 mg sodium, 45 g carbo., 6 g fiber, 26 g pro.

beer-braised BEEF SHORT RIBS

Who would have known that beer, molasses, and balsamic vinegar are flavors that would make meat taste amazing? Try it for yourself.

Prep: 15 minutes
Cook: 11 to 12 hours (low) or
        5½ to 6 hours (high)
Makes: 4 to 6 servings

- 5 **pounds beef short ribs**
- 1 **14-ounce can beef broth**
- 1 **12-ounce can dark beer**
- 1 **medium onion, cut into thin wedges**
- ¼ **cup molasses**
- 2 **tablespoons balsamic vinegar**
- 1 **teaspoon dried thyme, crushed**
- 1 **teaspoon bottled hot pepper sauce**
- ½ **teaspoon salt**
- **Mashed potatoes or hot buttered noodles (optional)**
- **Fresh thyme leaves (optional)**

1 Place ribs in a 5- to 6-quart slow cooker. Add broth, beer, onion, molasses, vinegar, dried thyme, hot pepper sauce, and salt.

2 Cover and cook on low-heat setting for 11 to 12 hours or on high-heat setting for 5½ to 6 hours.

3 Using a slotted spoon, transfer ribs to a serving platter. Cover and keep warm. Skim off fat from cooking liquid. Serve cooking liquid with ribs for dipping. If desired, serve ribs with mashed potatoes and garnish with fresh thyme leaves.

Nutrition facts per serving: 481 cal., 19 g total fat (8 g sat. fat), 132 mg chol., 821 mg sodium, 22 g carbo., 0 g fiber, 46 g pro.

short RIBS OVER GORGONZOLA POLENTA

To make the polenta ahead, before adding the cheese, cover the cooled polenta and hold at room temperature for a couple of hours or chill for several hours. Reheat and add the cheese.

Prep: 20 minutes + 30 minutes (for polenta)
Cook: 9 to 10 hours (low) or 4½ to 5 hours (high)
Makes: 6 servings

2½ to 3 pounds boneless beef short ribs

2 large onions, cut into thin wedges

1 cup thinly sliced carrots (2 medium)

1 medium fennel bulb, cored and cut into thin wedges

1 14.5-ounce can diced tomatoes, undrained

1 cup dry red wine

2 tablespoons quick-cooking tapioca, crushed

2 tablespoons tomato paste

1 teaspoon dried rosemary, crushed

1 teaspoon salt

½ teaspoon ground black pepper

4 cloves garlic, minced
   Gorgonzola Polenta*

1 Trim fat from meat. In a 5- to 6-quart slow cooker, combine onions, carrots, and fennel. Top with meat.

2 In a small bowl, combine tomatoes, wine, tapioca, tomato paste, rosemary, salt, pepper, and garlic. Pour over mixture in cooker.

3 Cover and cook on low-heat setting for 9 to 10 hours or on high-heat setting for 4½ to 5 hours.

4 Meanwhile, prepare Gorgonzola Polenta. To serve, spoon polenta into shallow bowls. Spoon meat and vegetable mixture over polenta.

*Gorgonzola Polenta: In a large saucepan, bring 2½ cups water to boiling. Meanwhile, in a bowl stir together 1 cup coarse-ground yellow cornmeal, 1 cup cold water, and ½ teaspoon salt. Slowly add cornmeal mixture to boiling water, stirring constantly. Cook and stir until mixture returns to boiling. Reduce heat to medium low. Cook for 25 to 30 minutes or until very thick, stirring frequently and adjusting heat as necessary to maintain a very slow boil. Stir in ⅓ cup crumbled Gorgonzola cheese or other blue cheese.

Nutrition facts per serving: 489 cal., 18 g total fat (8 g sat. fat), 113 mg chol., 1121 mg sodium, 32 g carbo., 4 g fiber, 41 g pro.

swedish MEATBALLS

Aside from a streamlined prep time—thanks to convenience products—this is a traditional take on the classic. Fans of this dish wouldn't want it any other way.

Prep: 20 minutes
Cook: 5 to 6 hours (low) or
      2½ to 3 hours (high)
Makes: 10 servings

- 2 12-ounce jars beef gravy
- 3 4.5-ounce jars (drained weight) sliced mushrooms, drained
- 1 large onion, cut into wedges
- 1 tablespoon Worcestershire sauce
- ¼ teaspoon ground allspice
- 2 16-ounce packages frozen cooked plain meatballs, thawed
- 1 8-ounce carton sour cream
- 6 cups hot cooked noodles
   Snipped fresh parsley (optional)

1 In a 4½- or 5-quart slow cooker, combine gravy, mushrooms, onion, Worcestershire sauce, and allspice. Stir in meatballs.

2 Cover and cook on low-heat setting for 5 to 6 hours or on high-heat setting for 2½ to 3 hours.

3 In a small bowl, gradually stir about ½ cup of the hot gravy mixture into sour cream. Add sour cream mixture to cooker, stirring gently until combined. Serve meatball mixture over hot cooked noodles. If desired, sprinkle with parsley.

Nutrition facts per serving: 503 cal., 31 g total fat (14 g sat. fat), 76 mg chol., 1240 mg sodium, 37 g carbo., 4 g fiber, 20 g pro.

spicy STEAK AND BEANS

Queso fresco (KAY-so FRESK-o) means "fresh cheese" in Spanish, and you can find it in large supermarkets and Mexican food stores.

Prep: 25 minutes
Cook: 7 to 9 hours (low) or
       3½ to 4½ hours (high);
       + 30 minutes (high)
Makes: 6 servings

1½ **pounds beef flank steak**

1 **10-ounce can chopped tomatoes with green chile peppers, undrained**

½ **cup chopped onion**

2 **cloves garlic, minced**

1 **tablespoon snipped fresh oregano or 1 teaspoon dried oregano, crushed**

1 **teaspoon chili powder**

1 **teaspoon ground cumin**

¼ **teaspoon salt**

¼ **teaspoon ground black pepper**

2 **small green, red, and/or yellow sweet peppers, cut into strips**

1 **15-ounce can pinto beans, rinsed and drained**

   Hot cooked brown rice (optional)

   Crumbled queso fresco or feta cheese (optional)

1 Trim fat from meat. Place meat in a 3½- or 4-quart slow cooker. In a bowl, stir together undrained tomatoes, onion, garlic, dried oregano (if using), chili powder, cumin, salt, and black pepper. Pour over meat.

2 Cover and cook on low-heat setting for 7 to 9 hours or on high-heat setting for 3½ to 4½ hours.

3 If using low-heat setting, turn to high-heat setting. Stir in sweet pepper strips and pinto beans. Cover and cook for 30 minutes more. Remove meat; cool slightly. Shred or thinly slice meat across the grain. Stir fresh oregano (if using) into bean mixture.

4 If desired, spoon rice into soup bowls. Arrange meat on top of rice. Spoon bean mixture over meat. If desired, sprinkle with cheese.

Nutrition facts per serving: 262 cal., 8 g total fat (3 g sat. fat), 45 mg chol., 452 mg sodium, 17 g carbo., 4 g fiber, 29 g pro.

sloppy JOES WITH A KICK

There's nothing ho-hum about this familiar favorite! Sassy ingredients give it a lively twist.

Prep: 20 minutes
Cook: 6 to 8 hours (low) or
      3 to 4 hours (high)
Makes: 8 servings

1½ **pounds lean ground beef**

 1 **cup chopped onion**

 1 **clove garlic, minced**

 1 **6-ounce can vegetable juice**

 ½ **cup ketchup**

 ½ **cup water**

 2 **tablespoons no-calorie,
     heat-stable granular sugar
     substitute**

 2 **tablespoons chopped, canned
     jalapeño chile peppers
     (optional)**

 1 **tablespoon prepared mustard**

 2 **teaspoons chili powder**

 1 **teaspoon Worcestershire
     sauce**

 8 **whole wheat hamburger
     buns, split and toasted**

    **Shredded reduced-fat
     cheddar cheese (optional)**

    **Sweet pepper strips
     (optional)**

1 In a large skillet, cook ground beef, onion, and garlic until meat is brown and onion is tender. Drain off fat.

2 Meanwhile, in a 3½- or 4-quart slow cooker combine vegetable juice, ketchup, water, sugar substitute, jalapeño peppers (if desired), mustard, chili powder, and Worcestershire sauce. Stir in meat mixture.

3 Cover and cook on low-heat setting for 6 to 8 hours or on high-heat setting for 3 to 4 hours. Spoon meat mixture onto bun halves. If desired, sprinkle with cheese and serve with sweet pepper strips.

Nutrition facts per serving: 310 cal., 13 g total fat (5 g sat. fat), 53 mg chol., 522 mg sodium, 27 g carbo., 3 g fiber, 21 g pro.

round STEAK WITH HERBS

Cream of celery soup is the flavor base in this beef recipe. If you like, try other soup varieties such as cream of mushroom or onion.

Prep: 10 minutes
Cook: 10 to 12 hours (low) or
5 to 6 hours (high)
Makes: 6 servings

2 **pounds beef round steak, cut ¾ inch thick**

1 **medium onion, sliced**

1 **10.75-ounce can condensed cream of celery soup**

½ **teaspoon dried oregano, crushed**

¼ **teaspoon dried thyme, crushed**

¼ **teaspoon ground black pepper**

Hot cooked whole wheat pasta (optional)

1 Trim fat from meat. Cut steak into serving-size portions. Place onion in a 3½- or 4-quart slow cooker; place meat on top of onion. In a small bowl, combine soup, oregano, thyme, and pepper; pour over meat.

2 Cover and cook on low-heat setting for 10 to 12 hours or on high-heat setting for 5 to 6 hours. If desired, serve steak with hot cooked pasta.

Nutrition facts per serving: 249 cal., 9 g total fat (3 g sat. fat), 78 mg chol., 475 mg sodium, 5 g carbo., 1 g fiber, 34 g pro.

easy BEEF BURGUNDY

The canned soups and onion soup mix do most of the work—all you have to do is cut up the meat and mushrooms.

Prep: 20 minutes
Cook: 8 to 10 hours (low) or
     4 to 5 hours (high)
Makes: 6 servings

1½ **pounds beef stew meat, trimmed and cut into 1-inch pieces**

2 **tablespoons cooking oil**

1 **10.75-ounce can reduced-fat and reduced-sodium condensed cream of celery soup**

1 **10.75-ounce can reduced-fat and reduced-sodium condensed cream of mushroom soup**

¾ **cup Burgundy**

1 **envelope (½ of a 2-ounce package) onion soup mix**

3 **cups sliced fresh mushrooms (8 ounces)**

    Hot cooked whole wheat pasta or brown rice (optional)

① In a large skillet, brown meat, half at a time, in hot oil. Drain off fat. In a 3½- to 5-quart slow cooker, combine celery soup, mushroom soup, Burgundy, and onion soup mix. Stir in meat and mushrooms.

② Cover and cook on low-heat setting for 8 to 10 hours or on high-heat setting for 4 to 5 hours. If desired, serve over hot cooked pasta.

Nutrition facts per serving: 301 cal., 13 g total fat (3 g sat. fat), 58 mg chol., 628 mg sodium, 12 g carbo., 0 g fiber, 27 g pro.

Wine for Flavor

Cooking with wine is a great way to boost flavor without adding fat and with few extra calories. Common knowledge dictates the use of cheap, not necessarily great-tasting, wine in cooking, but you might want to rethink this advice. When you cook with wine, the liquid evaporates, leaving a more concentrated flavor. Of course you don't need to break the bank, but you should at least use wine that you like to be sure you'll enjoy the stronger flavor brought out by the cooking.

so-easy PEPPER STEAK

In the mood for Mexican, Cajun, or Italian? Choose the appropriately seasoned tomatoes for robust flavor that usually comes only from a long list of seasonings.

Prep: 15 minutes
Cook: 10 to 12 hours (low) or
5 to 6 hours (high)
Makes: 8 servings

2 **pounds boneless beef round steak, cut ¾ to 1 inch thick**

Salt

Ground black pepper

1 **14.5-ounce can Cajun-, Mexican-, or Italian-style stewed tomatoes, undrained**

⅓ **cup Italian-style tomato paste**

½ **teaspoon bottled hot pepper sauce**

1 **16-ounce package frozen sweet pepper stir-fry vegetables (yellow, green, and red peppers and onion)**

Hot cooked noodles or hot mashed potatoes

1 Trim fat from meat. Cut meat into serving-size pieces. Lightly sprinkle with salt and black pepper. Place meat in a 3½- or 4-quart slow cooker. In a medium bowl, combine tomatoes, tomato paste, and hot pepper sauce. Pour over meat in cooker. Add frozen vegetables.

2 Cover and cook on low-heat setting for 10 to 12 hours or on high-heat setting for 5 to 6 hours. Serve over hot cooked noodles.

Nutrition facts per serving: 303 cal., 6 g total fat (2 g sat. fat), 80 mg chol., 416 mg sodium, 29 g carbo., 2 g fiber, 30 g pro.

beef WITH MUSHROOMS

Cook a package of frozen mashed potatoes to serve with this saucy round steak. If you like, stir snipped fresh basil or grated Parmesan cheese into the cooked potatoes.

Prep: 10 minutes
Cook: 8 to 10 hours (low) or
      4 to 5 hours (high)
Makes: 4 servings

- 1 **pound boneless beef round steak, cut 1 inch thick**
- 1 **medium onion, sliced**
- 1 **4-ounce jar whole mushrooms, drained**
- 1 **12-ounce jar beef gravy**
- ¼ **cup water**

1 Trim fat from meat. Cut meat into serving-size pieces. Place onion slices in a 3½- or 4-quart slow cooker. Arrange mushrooms over onions; add beef. In a small bowl, stir together gravy and water. Pour over beef.

2 Cover and cook on low-heat setting for 8 to 10 hours or on high-heat setting for 4 to 5 hours.

Nutrition facts per serving: 193 cal., 4 g total fat (2 g sat. fat), 47 mg chol., 744 mg sodium, 9 g carbo., 2 g fiber, 29 g pro.

brisket IN ALE

The flavorful gravy—made from the beer-spiked cooking liquid—is the finishing touch to this tender meat dish.

Prep: 25 minutes
Cook: 10 to 12 hours (low) or
      5 to 6 hours (high);
      + 10 minutes
Makes: 10 servings

- 1 **3- to 4-pound fresh beef brisket**
- 2 **medium onions, thinly sliced and separated into rings**
- 1 **bay leaf**
- 1 **12-ounce can beer**
- ¼ **cup chili sauce**
- 2 **tablespoons no-calorie, heat-stable granular sugar substitute**
- ½ **teaspoon dried thyme, crushed**
- ¼ **teaspoon salt**
- ¼ **teaspoon ground black pepper**
- 1 **clove garlic, minced**
- 2 **tablespoons cornstarch**
- 2 **tablespoons cold water**

1 Trim fat from meat. If necessary, cut brisket to fit into a 3½- to 6-quart slow cooker. Place the onions, bay leaf, and brisket in the cooker. In a medium bowl, combine beer, chili sauce, sugar substitute, thyme, salt, pepper, and garlic; pour over meat.

2 Cover and cook on low-heat setting for 10 to 12 hours or on high-heat setting for 5 to 6 hours.

3 Using a slotted spoon, transfer brisket and onions to a serving platter; cover with foil to keep warm. Discard bay leaf.

4 For gravy, pour juices into a large measuring cup; skim fat. Measure 2½ cups liquid; discard remaining liquid. In a medium saucepan, stir together cornstarch and water; stir in the cooking liquid. Cook and stir until thickened and bubbly; cook and stir for 2 minutes more. Pass gravy with meat.

Nutrition facts per serving: 170 cal., 6 g total fat (2 g sat. fat), 46 mg chol., 216 mg sodium, 6 g carbo., 1 g fiber, 20 g pro.

super-simple BEEF STEW

Super-simple is right. It's hard to believe so few ingredients add up to such a satisfying one-dish winner.

Prep: 15 minutes
Cook: 8 to 9 hours (low) or
4 to 4½ hours (high);
+ 10 minutes on high
Makes: 4 servings

12 ounces small red potatoes, quartered (about 2 cups)

4 medium carrots, cut into ½-inch pieces

1 small red onion, cut into wedges

1 pound beef stew meat

1 10.75-ounce can condensed cream of mushroom or cream of celery soup

1 cup beef broth

½ teaspoon dried marjoram or dried thyme, crushed

1 9-ounce package frozen cut green beans, thawed

1 In a 3½- or 4-quart slow cooker, place potatoes, carrots, onion, stew meat, soup, beef broth, and marjoram. Stir to combine.

2 Cover and cook on low-heat setting for 8 to 9 hours or on high-heat setting for 4 to 4½ hours.

3 If using low-heat setting, turn to high-heat setting. Stir in thawed green beans. Cover and cook for 10 to 15 minutes more or just until green beans are tender.

Nutrition facts per serving: 365 cal., 13 g total fat (4 g sat. fat), 54 mg chol., 830 mg sodium, 32 g carbo., 6 g fiber, 31 g pro.

tex-mex MAC AND CHEESE

Please the kids at the potluck with this entrée. Macaroni and cheese with taco flavorings combines two of their favorite foods into one delish dish.

Prep: 20 minutes
Cook: 5½ to 6 hours (low)
Makes: 10 servings

- 2 **pounds lean ground beef**
- 1 **cup chopped onion (1 large)**
- 3 **cups shredded Mexican-blend cheese (12 ounces)**
- 1 **16-ounce jar salsa**
- 1 **15-ounce jar cheese dip**
- 1 **4-ounce can diced green chile peppers, undrained**
- 1 **2.25-ounce can sliced pitted black olives, drained**
- 12 **ounces dried elbow macaroni**

1 In a large skillet, cook ground beef and onion until meat is brown and onion is tender. Drain off fat. Place meat mixture in a 4½- to 6-quart slow cooker. Add Mexican-blend cheese, salsa, cheese dip, chile peppers, and olives; stir to combine.

2 Cover and cook on low-heat setting for 5½ to 6 hours (do not use high-heat setting).

3 Meanwhile, cook macaroni according to package directions; drain. Stir macaroni into mixture in cooker.

Nutrition facts per serving: 577 cal., 32 g total fat (17 g sat. fat), 113 mg chol., 1337 mg sodium, 36 g carbo., 2 g fiber, 35 g pro.

barbecue PORK RIBS

No need to fire up the grill for these sassy barbecued ribs—they just simmer away in your slow cooker. If you have any leftovers, shred the meat to make sandwiches.

Prep: 25 minutes
Cook: 10 to 12 hours (low) or
      5 to 6 hours (high)
Makes: 4 to 6 servings

3 **to 3½ pounds pork country-style ribs**
1 **cup ketchup**
½ **cup finely chopped onion**
¼ **cup packed brown sugar**
1 **tablespoon Worcestershire sauce**
½ **teaspoon chili powder**
½ **teaspoon liquid smoke**
¼ **teaspoon garlic powder**
¼ **teaspoon bottled hot pepper sauce**

1 Place ribs in a 3½- or 4-quart slow cooker. In a small bowl, combine ketchup, onion, brown sugar, Worcestershire sauce, chili powder, liquid smoke, garlic powder, and hot pepper sauce. Pour over ribs in cooker, turning ribs to coat.

2 Cover and cook on low-heat setting for 10 to 12 hours or on high-heat setting for 5 to 6 hours.

3 Transfer ribs to a platter; cover to keep warm. Skim fat from surface of sauce; pour sauce into a medium saucepan. Bring sauce to boiling; reduce heat slightly. Boil gently, uncovered, for 5 to 7 minutes or until thickened to desired consistency (should make about 1 cup). Pass sauce with ribs.

Nutrition facts per serving: 419 cal., 15 g total fat (5 g sat. fat), 121 mg chol., 891 mg sodium, 33 g carbo., 2 g fiber, 38 g pro.

peach-glazed PORK ROAST WITH CORN BREAD STUFFING

Fruit-studded stuffing topped with a peach-glazed roast—now that's a meal to savor!

Prep: 25 minutes
Cook: 5 to 6 hours (low) or
2½ to 3 hours (high)
Makes: 8 servings

Nonstick cooking spray

1 **2- to 2½-pound boneless pork top loin roast (single loin)**

Salt

Ground black pepper

1 **tablespoon cooking oil**

4 **cups corn bread stuffing mix**

¾ **cup reduced-sodium chicken broth**

½ **cup mixed dried fruit bits**

¼ **cup chopped onion**

½ **cup peach spreadable fruit**

1 **teaspoon finely shredded lemon peel**

¼ **teaspoon ground cinnamon**

1 Lightly coat a 3½- or 4-quart slow cooker with cooking spray. Trim fat from meat. If necessary, cut meat to fit into cooker. Sprinkle meat with salt and pepper. In a large skillet, brown meat on all sides in hot oil. Drain off fat. Set aside.

2 In a large bowl, toss together stuffing mix, broth, dried fruit, and onion. Place stuffing mixture in prepared cooker. Add meat. In a small bowl, stir together peach spreadable fruit, lemon peel, and cinnamon. Spread over meat in cooker.

3 Cover and cook on low-heat setting for 5 to 6 hours or on high-heat setting for 2½ to 3 hours.

4 Remove meat from cooker. Slice meat. Stir stuffing; serve with meat.

Nutrition facts per serving: 408 cal., 9 g total fat (2 g sat. fat), 67 mg chol., 639 mg sodium, 52 g carbo., 0 g fiber, 29 g pro.

italian PORK WITH MASHED SWEET POTATOES

A fennel seed rub coats this pork with extraordinary licorice-like flavor, while the golden-orange potatoes add just the right amount of sweetness.

Prep: 20 minutes
Cook: 8 to 10 hours (low) or
      4 to 5 hours (high)
Makes: 4 servings

- 1 **teaspoon fennel seeds, crushed**
- ½ **teaspoon dried oregano, crushed**
- ½ **teaspoon garlic powder**
- ½ **teaspoon paprika**
- ¼ **teaspoon salt**
- ¼ **teaspoon ground black pepper**
- 1 **1½- to 2-pound boneless pork shoulder roast**
- 1 **pound sweet potatoes, peeled and cut into 1-inch pieces**
- 1 **cup chicken broth**

1. In a small bowl, combine fennel seeds, oregano, garlic powder, paprika, salt, and pepper. Trim fat from meat. Sprinkle fennel seed mixture evenly over meat; rub in with your fingers. If necessary, cut meat to fit into a 3½- or 4-quart slow cooker.

2. Place sweet potatoes in cooker. Add meat. Pour broth over mixture in cooker.

3. Cover and cook on low-heat setting for 8 to 10 hours or on high-heat setting for 4 to 5 hours.

4. Remove meat from cooker, reserving cooking juices. Slice meat. Using a slotted spoon, transfer sweet potatoes to a medium bowl. Use a potato masher to mash sweet potatoes, adding some of the cooking juices, if necessary, to moisten. Serve meat with mashed sweet potatoes.

Nutrition facts per serving: 356 cal., 14 g total fat (5 g sat. fat), 115 mg chol., 525 mg sodium, 21 g carbo., 3 g fiber, 35 g pro.

texas TWO-STEP STEW

Serve this wake-your-taste buds stew with warm flour tortillas, cool sour cream, and tangy lime wedges.

Prep: 20 minutes
Cook: 4 to 6 hours (low),
        + 1 hour, or 2 to 3 hours
        (high), + 45 minutes
Makes: 6 servings

 8 ounces uncooked chorizo
    sausage (remove casings
    if present)

 1 medium onion, chopped

 1 15-ounce can Mexican or
    Tex-Mex-style chili beans,
    undrained

 1 15-ounce can hominy or one
    11-ounce can whole kernel
    corn with sweet peppers,
    drained

 1 6-ounce package regular
    Spanish-style rice mix

 6 cups water

1 In a medium skillet, cook sausage and onion over medium heat until sausage is brown. Drain off fat. Transfer sausage mixture to a 3½- or 4-quart slow cooker. Stir in undrained chili beans, hominy, and, if present, the seasoning packet contents from the rice mix (set aside remaining rice mix). Pour the water over all. Cover and cook on low-heat setting for 4 to 6 hours or on high-heat setting for 2 to 3 hours.

2 Stir in remaining rice mix. Cover and cook on low-heat setting for 1 hour more or on high-heat setting for 45 minutes more.

Nutrition facts per serving: 383 cal., 16 g total fat (6 g sat. fat), 33 mg chol., 1,385 mg sodium, 44 g carbo., 6 g fiber, 16 g pro.

sweet-sour PORK STEW

Sweet-and-sour pork can be a lot of work to prepare because the pork is battered and fried. With this easy-to-make stew, you can enjoy all the same flavors but skip the kitchen time.

Prep: 25 minutes
Cook: 7 to 9 hours (low) or
      3½ to 4½ hours (high)
Makes: 4 to 6 servings

1½ **pounds lean pork stew meat**

 3 **tablespoons all-purpose flour**

½ **teaspoon salt**

¼ **teaspoon ground black pepper**

 1 **tablespoon cooking oil**

 1 **cup chopped onion**

 5 **medium carrots, cut into**
   ½-inch-thick slices

 1 **14.5-ounce can diced**
   tomatoes, undrained

¼ **cup packed brown sugar**

¼ **cup vinegar**

 2 **tablespoons quick-cooking**
   tapioca

 1 **tablespoon Worcestershire**
   sauce

1 Cut meat into 1-inch pieces. In a resealable plastic bag, combine flour, salt, and pepper. Add meat pieces, a few at a time, shaking to coat. In a large skillet, cook half of the meat in hot oil until brown. Transfer meat to a 3½- or 4-quart slow cooker. Add remaining meat and the onion to skillet. Cook until meat is brown and onion is tender. Drain off fat. Transfer meat mixture to cooker. Add carrots.

2 In a medium bowl, combine undrained tomatoes, brown sugar, vinegar, tapioca, and Worcestershire sauce. Pour over mixture in cooker.

3 Cover and cook on low-heat setting for 7 to 9 hours or on high-heat setting for 3½ to 4½ hours.

Nutrition facts per serving: 394 cal., 10 g total fat (3 g sat. fat), 95 mg chol., 619 mg sodium, 41 g carbo., 4 g fiber, 34 g pro.

pork WITH PARSNIPS AND PEARS

Bartlett and Bosc pears work well with this pork roast because they hold their shape during cooking.

Prep: 30 minutes
Cook: 11 to 12 hours (low) or
       5½ to 6 hours (high)
Makes: 8 to 10 servings

- 1   2½- to 3-pound boneless pork top loin roast (single loin)
- 1   tablespoon cooking oil
- 1½ pounds parsnips and/or carrots, peeled and cut into 1½- to 2-inch pieces*
- 2   medium pears, peeled, quartered, and cored (stems intact, if desired; about 2 cups)
- 2   tablespoons quick-cooking tapioca
- 1   tablespoon bottled minced garlic or 6 cloves garlic, minced
- 1   teaspoon dried rosemary, crushed
- 1   teaspoon dried thyme, crushed
- ½   teaspoon salt
- ¼   teaspoon ground black pepper
- ½   cup port wine or apple juice
      Salt
      Ground black pepper

1 In a large skillet, brown meat on all sides in hot oil. Place parsnips and/or carrots and pears in a 5- to 6-quart slow cooker; sprinkle with tapioca. Place meat on top of parsnips and pears; sprinkle meat with garlic, rosemary, thyme, the ½ teaspoon salt, and the ¼ teaspoon pepper. Pour wine over all.

2 Cover and cook on low-heat setting for 11 to 12 hours or on high-heat setting for 5½ to 6 hours.

3 Transfer meat to serving platter, reserving cooking liquid; use a slotted spoon to transfer parsnips and/or carrots and pears to serving platter.

4 Slice meat. Season sauce to taste with salt and pepper. Serve with meat, vegetables, and pears.

***Note:** Cut any thick carrot or parsnip pieces in half lengthwise.

Nutrition facts per serving: 340 cal., 9 g total fat (3 g sat. fat), 78 mg chol., 292 mg sodium, 27 g carbo., 6 g fiber, 32 g pro.

apricot PULLED PORK

Prep: 20 minutes
Cook: 8 to 10 hours (low) or
        4 to 5 hours (high)
Makes: 8 servings

Nonstick cooking spray

1   **3- to 3½-pound boneless pork
    shoulder roast**

1   **10-ounce jar apricot
    spreadable fruit**

1   **cup bottled hot-style
    barbecue sauce**

½   **cup chopped sweet onion
    (such as Vidalia, Maui, or
    Walla Walla)**

½   **cup snipped dried apricots**

8   **kaiser rolls or hamburger
    buns**

1 Lightly coat a 3½- or 4-quart slow cooker with cooking spray. Trim fat from meat. If necessary, cut meat to fit into cooker. Place meat in prepared cooker. In a medium bowl, combine spreadable fruit, barbecue sauce, onion, and dried apricots. Pour over meat in cooker.

2 Cover and cook on low heat-setting for 8 to 10 hours or on high-heat setting for 4 to 5 hours.

3 Transfer meat to a cutting board. Using two forks, gently shred the meat. In a large bowl, combine shredded meat and some of the sauce from the cooker. Serve meat mixture on kaiser rolls. Pass remaining sauce.

Nutrition facts per serving: 553 cal., 17 g total fat (5 g sat. fat), 116 mg chol., 685 mg sodium, 61 g carbo., 2 g fiber, 40 g pro.

ham AND SCALLOPED POTATOES

This old-fashioned favorite has been updated for today's busy cooks with frozen hash browns, canned soup, and ham and pimiento purchased already diced. It goes together in minutes but simmers slow and easy all day.

Prep: 10 minutes
Cook: 7 to 9 hours (low) or
         3½ to 4 hours (high)
Makes: 6 servings

- 1 **28-ounce package loose-pack frozen hash brown potatoes with onion and peppers**
- 2 **cups diced cooked ham (10 ounces)**
- 1 **2-ounce jar diced pimiento, drained**
- ¼ **teaspoon ground black pepper**
- 1 **11-ounce can condensed cheddar cheese soup**
- ¾ **cup milk**
- 1 **tablespoon snipped fresh parsley**

1 In a 3½-quart slow cooker, combine frozen hash brown potatoes, ham, pimiento, and pepper.

2 In a medium bowl, combine cheddar cheese soup and milk; pour over the potato mixture in cooker. Stir to combine.

3 Cover and cook on low-heat setting for 7 to 9 hours or on high-heat setting for 3½ to 4 hours. Stir in parsley.

Nutrition facts per serving: 241 cal., 9 g total fat (3 g sat. fat), 37 mg chol., 1,180 mg sodium, 30 g carbo., 3 g fiber, 16 g pro.

potatoes, SAUERKRAUT, AND SAUSAGE SUPPER

Some good crusty bread and a selection of your favorite mustards are perfect serve-alongs for this robust, German-style meal.

Prep: 20 minutes
Cook: 5 to 6 hours (low) or
      2½ to 3 hours (high),
      + 30 minutes on high
Makes: 8 servings

- 1 **20-ounce package refrigerated diced potatoes with onions**
- 1 **cup chopped green sweet pepper**
- 1 **cup chopped carrot**
- 1½ **pounds cooked smoked Polish sausage, cut into 2-inch pieces**
- ⅔ **cup apple juice or apple cider**
- 1 **tablespoon cider vinegar**
- ½ **teaspoon caraway seeds**
- ¼ **teaspoon salt**
- ¼ **teaspoon ground black pepper**
- 1 **14- to 16-ounce can sauerkraut, drained**

1 In a 4½- to 5½-quart slow cooker, combine potatoes, sweet pepper, and carrot. Add sausage.

2 In a small bowl, stir together apple juice, cider vinegar, caraway seeds, salt, and black pepper. Pour over mixture in cooker.

3 Cover and cook on low-heat setting for 5 to 6 hours or on high-heat setting for 2½ to 3 hours.

4 If using low-heat setting, turn to high-heat setting. Stir in sauerkraut. Cover and cook for 30 minutes more. To serve, transfer mixture to a serving bowl.

Nutrition facts per serving: 374 cal., 25 g total fat (9 g sat. fat), 60 mg chol., 1,291 mg sodium, 24 g carbo., 4 g fiber, 14 g pro.

pork CHOPS WITH ORANGE-DIJON SAUCE

Orange marmalade laced with Dijon mustard provides a sweet yet snappy glaze for these boneless chops.

Prep: 15 minutes
Cook: 6 to 7 hours (low) or
     3 to 3½ hours (high)
Makes: 6 servings

- 6 **boneless pork sirloin chops, cut 1 inch thick**
- **Salt**
- **Ground black pepper**
- ½ **teaspoon dried thyme, crushed**
- 1 **cup orange marmalade**
- ⅓ **cup Dijon-style mustard**
- ¼ **cup water**

1 Sprinkle chops lightly with salt and pepper. Sprinkle chops with thyme. Place chops in a 3½- or 4-quart slow cooker. In a small bowl, combine orange marmalade and mustard. Remove 2 tablespoons of the marmalade mixture; cover and refrigerate. Stir the water into remaining marmalade mixture. Pour over chops in cooker.

2 Cover and cook on low-heat setting for 6 to 7 hours or on high-heat setting for 3 to 3½ hours.

3 Transfer chops to a serving platter, discarding the cooking liquid. Spread reserved marmalade mixture over chops.

Nutrition facts per serving: 409 cal., 15 g total fat (5 g sat. fat), 166 mg chol., 212 mg sodium, 9 g carbo., 1 g fiber, 56 g pro.

seeded PORK ROAST

A savory blend of anise, fennel, caraway, dill, and celery seeds creates a crustlike coating for this ultratender pork roast. The cooking liquid contains apple juice, which lends a subtle sweetness.

Prep: 25 minutes
Cook: 9 to 11 hours (low) or
      4½ to 5½ hours (high);
      + 10 minutes (high)
Makes: 8 servings

- 1 2½- to 3-pound boneless pork shoulder roast
- 1 tablespoon soy sauce
- 2 teaspoons anise seeds, crushed
- 2 teaspoons fennel seeds, crushed
- 2 teaspoons caraway seeds, crushed
- 2 teaspoons dill seeds, crushed
- 2 teaspoons celery seeds, crushed
- ½ cup beef broth
- ⅔ cup apple juice
- 1 tablespoon cornstarch

1 Remove netting from roast, if present. If necessary, cut roast to fit into a 3½- to 5-quart slow cooker. Trim fat from meat. Brush soy sauce over surface of roast. On a large piece of foil, combine the anise seeds, fennel seeds, caraway seeds, dill seeds, and celery seeds. Roll roast in seeds to coat evenly.

2 Place roast in cooker. Pour broth and ⅓ cup of the apple juice around roast.

3 Cover and cook on low-heat setting for 9 to 11 hours or on high-heat setting for 4½ to 5½ hours.

4 Transfer roast to a serving platter. For gravy, strain cooking juices and skim fat; transfer juices to small saucepan. Combine remaining apple juice and cornstarch; add to juices in saucepan. Cook and stir until thickened and bubbly. Cook and stir for 2 minutes more. Pass gravy with roast.

Nutrition facts per serving: 220 cal., 9 g total fat (3 g sat. fat), 92 mg chol., 285 mg sodium, 5 g carbo., 0 g fiber, 29 g pro.

hot PEPPER PORK SANDWICHES

You can adjust the heat level by varying the number of jalapeños you use. Want to turn up the heat even more? Don't seed the peppers before adding them.

Prep: 20 minutes
Cook: 11 to 12 hours (low) or
     5½ to 6 hours (high)
Makes: 8 servings

- 1 2½- to 3-pound boneless pork shoulder roast
- 2 teaspoons fajita seasoning
- 1 or 2 fresh jalapeño chile peppers, seeded, if desired, and finely chopped (see tip on page 25), or 1 large green or red sweet pepper, seeded and cut into bite-size strips
- 2 10-ounce cans enchilada sauce
- 8 whole grain hamburger buns or kaiser rolls, split and, if desired, toasted

1 Trim fat from meat. If necessary, cut roast to fit into a 3½- or 4-quart slow cooker. Place meat in the cooker. Sprinkle with fajita seasoning. Add peppers and enchilada sauce.

2 Cover and cook on low-heat setting for 11 to 12 hours or on high-heat setting for 5½ to 6 hours. Transfer roast to a cutting board. Using two forks, shred meat. Stir shredded meat into juices in slow cooker. Using a slotted spoon, spoon shredded meat mixture into toasted buns.

Nutrition facts per serving: 262 cal., 9 g total fat (3 g sat. fat), 58 mg chol., 778 mg sodium, 23 g carbo., 3 g fiber, 22 g pro.

thyme AND GARLIC CHICKEN

Thyme, garlic, a little orange juice, and a splash of balsamic vinegar flavor these moist, fork-tender chicken breasts.

Prep: 15 minutes
Cook: 5 to 6 hours (low) or
2½ to 3 hours (high);
+ 10 minutes
Makes: 6 to 8 servings

6 **cloves garlic, minced**

1½ **teaspoons dried thyme, crushed**

3 **to 4 pounds whole chicken breasts (with bone), halved and skinned**

¼ **cup orange juice**

1 **tablespoon balsamic vinegar**

1 Sprinkle garlic and thyme over chicken pieces. Place chicken in a 3½- or 4-quart slow cooker. Pour orange juice and vinegar over chicken.

2 Cover and cook on low-heat setting for 5 to 6 hours or on high-heat setting for 2½ to 3 hours.

3 Remove chicken from cooker; cover with foil to keep warm. Skim fat from cooking juices. Strain juices into a saucepan. Bring to boiling; reduce heat. Boil gently, uncovered, about 10 minutes or until reduced to 1 cup. Pass juices with chicken.

Nutrition facts per serving: 178 cal., 2 g total fat (0 g sat. fat), 85 mg chol., 78 mg sodium, 3 g carbo., 0 g fiber, 34 g pro.

mediterranean CHICKEN

If you think you've served chicken in every way imaginable, you'll love this dish. The flavors of artichokes, olives, and thyme lend a Mediterranean accent.

Prep: 20 minutes
Cook: 7 to 8 hours (low) or
3½ to 4 hours (high)
Makes: 6 servings

2 **cups sliced fresh mushrooms**

1 **14.5-ounce can diced tomatoes, undrained**

1 **8- or 9-ounce package frozen artichoke hearts**

1 **cup chicken broth**

½ **cup chopped onion**

½ **cup sliced, pitted ripe olives or ¼ cup capers, drained**

¼ **cup dry white wine or chicken broth**

3 **tablespoons quick-cooking tapioca**

2 **to 3 teaspoons curry powder**

¾ **teaspoon dried thyme, crushed**

¼ **teaspoon salt**

¼ **teaspoon ground black pepper**

1½ **pounds skinless, boneless chicken breast halves and/or thighs**

Hot cooked brown rice (optional)

1 In a 3½- or 4-quart slow cooker, place mushrooms, undrained tomatoes, frozen artichoke hearts, broth, onion, olives, and wine. Stir in tapioca, curry powder, thyme, salt, and pepper. Add chicken; spoon some of the tomato mixture over the chicken.

2 Cover and cook on low-heat setting for 7 to 8 hours or on high-heat setting for 3½ to 4 hours. If desired, serve with hot cooked rice.

Nutrition facts per serving: 227 cal., 4 g total fat (1 g sat. fat), 66 mg chol., 578 mg sodium, 15 g carbo., 4 g fiber, 29 g pro.

Oh, Tomato!

Canned tomatoes are a terrific pantry staple. They're available whole, pureed, diced, and seasoned. With few calories, tomatoes boost both the flavor and the nutritional impact of a dish. They're loaded with the antioxidant lycopene, which may prevent prostate cancer as well as other cancers and heart disease. Canned tomatoes, because they are cooked, have a much higher level of lycopene.

chicken IN WINE SAUCE

Chicken and hearty vegetables are simmered in a delicate wine-flavored sauce. Choose dark meat chicken—thighs or drumsticks—for this dish.

Prep: 20 minutes
Cook: 8 to 9 hours (low) or
  4 to 4½ hours (high);
  + 10 minutes
Makes: 6 servings

- 4 **medium red potatoes, quartered**
- 4 **medium carrots, cut into ½-inch pieces**
- 2 **stalks celery, cut into 1-inch pieces**
- 1 **small onion, sliced**
- 3 **pounds chicken thighs or drumsticks, skinned**
- 1 **tablespoon snipped fresh parsley**
- ½ **teaspoon salt**
- ½ **teaspoon dried rosemary, crushed**
- ½ **teaspoon dried thyme, crushed**
- ¼ **teaspoon ground black pepper**
- 1 **clove garlic, minced**
- 1 **cup chicken broth**
- ½ **cup dry white wine**
- 3 **tablespoons butter or margarine**
- 3 **tablespoons all-purpose flour**
  Snipped fresh thyme (optional)

1 In a 5- or 6-quart slow cooker, place potatoes, carrots, celery, and onion. Place chicken pieces on top of vegetables. Sprinkle with parsley, salt, rosemary, dried thyme, pepper, and garlic; add broth and wine.

2 Cover and cook on low-heat setting for 8 to 9 hours or on high-heat setting for 4 to 4½ hours. Using a slotted spoon, transfer chicken and vegetables to a serving platter; cover with foil to keep warm.

3 For gravy, skim fat from cooking juices; strain juices. In a large saucepan, melt butter. Stir in flour and cook for 1 minute. Add cooking juices. Cook and stir until thickened and bubbly. Cook and stir for 2 minutes more. If desired, sprinkle chicken and vegetables with snipped fresh thyme. Pass gravy with the chicken and vegetables.

Nutrition facts per serving: 328 cal., 11 g total fat (5 g sat. fat), 124 mg chol., 544 mg sodium, 24 g carbo., 3 g fiber, 29 g pro.

country CAPTAIN

The golden red sauce and fragrant spice blend bring your taste buds to attention even before the first bite of tender chicken.

Prep: 25 minutes
Cook: 5 to 6 hours (low) or
     2½ to 3 hours (high)
Makes: 6 servings

- 1 **medium sweet onion, cut into thin wedges**
- 3 **pounds chicken drumsticks and/or thighs, skinned**
- 1 **cup green sweet pepper strips (1 medium)**
- 1 **cup yellow sweet pepper strips (1 medium)**
- ¼ **cup dried currants or golden raisins**
- 2 **cloves garlic, minced**
- 1 **14-ounce can diced tomatoes, undrained**
- 2 **tablespoons quick-cooking tapioca, crushed**
- 2 **to 3 teaspoons curry powder**
- ½ **teaspoon salt**
- ½ **teaspoon ground cumin**
- ¼ **teaspoon ground mace**
- 3 **cups hot cooked rice**
- 2 **tablespoons chopped green onion (1)**
- 2 **tablespoons sliced almonds, toasted**

1 Place onion in a 3½- or 4-quart slow cooker. Add chicken, sweet peppers, currants, and garlic. In a large bowl, combine tomatoes, tapioca, curry powder, salt, cumin, and mace. Pour over mixture in cooker.

2 Cover and cook on low-heat setting for 5 to 6 hours or on high-heat setting for 2½ to 3 hours.

3 Serve over hot cooked rice. Sprinkle each serving with green onion and almonds.

Nutrition facts per serving: 338 cal., 6 g total fat (1 g sat. fat), 98 mg chol., 446 mg sodium, 40 g carbo., 4 g fiber, 31 g pro.

ginger-tomato CHICKEN

Chicken drumsticks and thighs are great for the slow cooker. They stay moist and tender during the long cooking time.

Prep: 20 minutes
Cook: 6 to 7 hours (low) or
      3 to 3½ hours (high)
Makes: 6 servings

12 **chicken drumsticks and/or thighs, skinned (2½ to 3 pounds)**

2 **14.5-ounce cans tomatoes**

2 **tablespoons quick-cooking tapioca**

1 **tablespoon grated fresh ginger**

1 **tablespoon snipped fresh cilantro or parsley**

4 **cloves garlic, minced**

2 **teaspoons brown sugar (optional)**

½ **teaspoon crushed red pepper**

½ **teaspoon salt**

    Hot cooked brown rice (optional)

1 Place chicken pieces in a 3½- or 4-quart slow cooker.

2 Drain 1 can of tomatoes; chop tomatoes from both cans. For sauce, in a medium bowl combine chopped tomatoes and the juice from 1 can, the tapioca, ginger, cilantro, garlic, brown sugar (if using), crushed red pepper, and salt. Pour sauce over chicken.

3 Cover and cook on low-heat setting for 6 to 7 hours or on high-heat setting for 3 to 3½ hours. Skim fat from sauce. Serve chicken with sauce in shallow bowls. If desired, serve with brown rice.

Nutrition facts per serving: 168 cal., 4 g total fat (1 g sat. fat), 81 mg chol., 472 mg sodium, 10 g carbo., 1 g fiber, 23 g pro.

italian CHICKEN AND PASTA

For a colorful variation, try spinach or red pepper fettuccine.

Prep: 15 minutes
Cook: 5 to 6 hours (low) or
          2½ to 3 hours (high)
Makes: 4 servings

12 ounces skinless, boneless
   chicken thighs

 1 9-ounce package frozen
   Italian-style green beans

 1 cup fresh mushrooms,
   quartered

 1 small onion, sliced ¼ inch
   thick

 1 14.5-ounce can Italian-style
   stewed tomatoes, undrained

 1 6-ounce can Italian-style
   tomato paste

 1 teaspoon dried Italian
   seasoning, crushed

 2 cloves garlic, minced

 6 ounces fettuccine, cooked
   and drained

 3 tablespoons finely shredded
   Parmesan cheese

1 Cut chicken into 1-inch pieces. In a 3½- or 4-quart slow cooker, place green beans, mushrooms, and onion. Place chicken on vegetables.

2 In a small bowl, combine undrained tomatoes, tomato paste, Italian seasoning, and garlic. Pour over chicken.

3 Cover and cook on low-heat setting for 5 to 6 hours or on high-heat setting for 2½ to 3 hours. Serve over hot cooked fettuccine. Sprinkle with Parmesan cheese.

Nutrition facts per serving: 405 cal., 7 g total fat (2 g sat. fat), 75 mg chol., 728 mg sodium, 55 g carbo., 4 g fiber, 28 g pro.

chicken OSSO BUCO

Prep: 45 minutes
Cook: 5 to 6 hours (low) or
      2½ to 3 hours (high)
Makes: 6 servings

- 2 **tablespoons all-purpose flour**
- ½ **teaspoon salt**
- ¼ **teaspoon ground black pepper**
- 12 **medium chicken drumsticks, skinned (about 3 pounds total)**
- 2 **tablespoons olive oil**
- 1 **cup chopped carrot**
- 1 **cup chopped onion**
- 1 **cup chopped celery**
- 6 **cloves garlic, minced**
- 2 **tablespoons quick-cooking tapioca**
- 1 **8-ounce can tomato sauce**
- ½ **cup dry white wine or chicken broth**
- ¼ **cup chicken broth**
- 1 **teaspoon finely shredded lemon peel**
- 1 **tablespoon lemon juice**
- 1 **teaspoon dried thyme, crushed**
- 3 **cups dried penne**

1 Place flour, salt, and black pepper in a resealable plastic bag. Add chicken, a few pieces at time, shaking to coat. In a 10-inch skillet, brown chicken, half at a time, in hot oil over medium heat about 10 minutes or until golden, turning once.

2 In a 4- to 5-quart slow cooker, combine carrot, onion, celery, and garlic. Sprinkle with tapioca. Place chicken on top of vegetables. In a medium bowl, stir together tomato sauce, wine, broth, lemon peel, lemon juice, and thyme; pour over chicken in cooker.

3 Cover and cook on low-heat setting for 5 to 6 hours or on high-heat setting for 2½ to 3 hours.

4 Prepare pasta according to package directions. Drain well. Spoon chicken and sauce over pasta.

Nutrition facts per serving: 407 cal., 9 g total fat (2 g sat. fat), 98 mg chol., 529 mg sodium, 42 g carbo., 3 g fiber, 33 g pro.

chicken AND DUMPLINGS

Prep: 25 minutes
Cook: 8 to 10 hours (low) or
       4 to 5 hours (high),
       + 25 minutes on high
Makes: 8 servings

  2 **cups chopped carrots**
  2 **cups chopped potatoes**
1½ **cups chopped parsnips**
  1 **clove garlic, minced**
  2 **bay leaves**
  1 **teaspoon dried sage, crushed**
  ¾ **teaspoon salt**
  ¼ **teaspoon ground black pepper**
  2 **pounds boneless, skinless
      chicken thighs, cut into
      1-inch pieces**
  1 **14-ounce can chicken broth**
  1 **10.75-ounce can condensed
      cream of chicken soup**
  2 **tablespoons water**
  1 **tablespoon cornstarch**
  ½ **cup all-purpose flour**
  ½ **cup shredded cheddar cheese
      (2 ounces)**
  ⅓ **cup cornmeal**
  1 **teaspoon baking powder**
  1 **egg, beaten**
  2 **tablespoons milk**
  2 **tablespoons butter, melted**

1 For stew, in a 4- or 5-quart slow cooker combine the carrots, potatoes, parsnips, garlic, bay leaves, sage, ½ teaspoon salt, and pepper. Place the chicken on top of the vegetables. In a medium bowl, gradually whisk broth into soup. Pour over chicken.

2 Cover and cook on low-heat setting for 8 to 10 hours or on high-heat setting for 4 to 5 hours.

3 If using low-heat setting, turn slow cooker to high-heat setting. With a wooden spoon, stir stew. Remove bay leaves; discard. In a small bowl, combine water and cornstarch; stir into stew until combined.

4 For dumplings, in a medium bowl combine flour, cheese, cornmeal, baking powder, and the remaining ¼ teaspoon salt. In a small bowl, combine egg, milk, and melted butter. Add egg mixture to flour mixture. Stir with a fork until moistened. Use 2 spoons to drop dough directly on top of stew.

5 Cover and cook for 25 to 30 minutes more or until a toothpick inserted into a dumpling comes out clean. (Do not lift cover during cooking.)

Nutrition facts per serving: 361 cal., 14 g total fat (6 g sat. fat), 140 mg chol., 948 mg sodium, 29 g carbo., 4 g fiber, 29 g pro.

chicken WITH SOURDOUGH-MUSHROOM STUFFING

If you like, use regular French bread instead.

Prep: 40 minutes
Cook: 4 to 5 hours (high)
Makes: 8 servings

Nonstick cooking spray

2 **tablespoons finely shredded lemon peel**

1 **tablespoon ground sage**

1 **tablespoon seasoned salt**

1½ **teaspoons ground black pepper**

8 **small chicken legs (drumstick-thigh portion), skinned (about 5 pounds total)**

¼ **cup butter**

4 **cups quartered or sliced fresh cremini, baby portobello, shiitake, and/or button mushrooms**

2 **cloves garlic, thinly sliced**

8 **cups sourdough baguette cut into 1-inch cubes (12 to 14 ounces)**

1 **cup coarsely shredded carrot**

1 **cup chicken broth**

¼ **cup chopped walnuts, toasted**

¼ **cup snipped fresh flat-leaf parsley**

❶ Lightly coat a 6-quart slow cooker with nonstick cooking spray. Set aside 1 teaspoon of the lemon peel. In a small bowl, combine the remaining 5 teaspoons lemon peel, the sage, seasoned salt, and pepper. Remove three-quarters of the sage mixture; sprinkle on the chicken legs and rub in with your fingers. Place chicken legs in the cooker.

❷ In a large skillet, melt butter over medium heat. Add mushrooms and garlic; cook and stir for 3 to 5 minutes or just until tender. Stir in remaining sage mixture. In a large bowl, combine bread cubes and carrot; add mushroom mixture. Drizzle with chicken broth; toss gently. Lightly pack stuffing on top of chicken in cooker. Cover and cook on high-heat setting for 4 to 5 hours.

❸ Using a slotted spoon, transfer stuffing and chicken to a serving platter; discard juices in cooker. In a small bowl, combine the reserved 1 teaspoon lemon peel, walnuts, and parsley; sprinkle on chicken.

Nutrition facts per serving: 412 cal., 17 g total fat (5 g sat. fat), 146 mg chol., 1,450 mg sodium, 27 g carbo., 3 g fiber, 39 g pro.

greek CHICKEN WITH COUSCOUS

Prep: 15 minutes
Cook: 5 to 6 hours (low) or
     2½ to 3 hours (high)
Stand: 5 minutes
Makes: 8 servings

2 **pounds skinless, boneless chicken breast halves**

2 **14½-ounce cans diced tomatoes with basil, oregano, and garlic, undrained**

1½ **cups water**

2 **6-ounce packages couscous with toasted pine nut mix**

1 **cup crumbled feta cheese (4 ounces)**

½ **cup pitted kalamata olives, coarsely chopped**

1 Cut chicken into ½-inch pieces. Place chicken in a 3½- or 4-quart slow cooker. Add undrained tomatoes and 1½ cups water.

2 Cover and cook on low-heat setting for 5 to 6 hours or on high-heat setting for 2½ to 3 hours. Stir in couscous. Cover and let stand for 5 minutes. Fluff couscous mixture with a fork.

3 To serve, spoon couscous mixture on each of 8 dinner plates. Sprinkle with feta cheese and olives.

Nutrition facts per serving: 377 cal., 8 g total fat (4 g sat. fat), 82 mg chol., 1,226 mg sodium, 41 g carbo., 3 g fiber, 36 g pro.

chicken AND VEGETABLES WITH HERBS

While fresh pearl onions need to be blanched and peeled, you can skip those steps with the frozen ones.

Prep: 20 minutes
Cook: 7 to 8 hours (low) or
3½ to 4 hours (high)
Makes: 4 servings

- 8 **ounces fresh mushrooms, halved**
- 1 **cup frozen pearl onions**
- ¾ **cup chicken broth**
- ¼ **cup dry red wine**
- 2 **tablespoons tomato paste**
- ½ **teaspoon garlic salt**
- ½ **teaspoon dried rosemary, crushed**
- ½ **teaspoon dried thyme, crushed**
- ¼ **teaspoon ground black pepper**
- 1 **bay leaf**
- 4 **small chicken legs (drumstick-thigh portion) skinned (2 to 2½ pounds total)**
- **Chicken broth (optional)**
- 2 **tablespoons all-purpose flour**
- **Hot cooked mashed potatoes (optional)**
- **Fresh parsley sprigs (optional)**

1 In a 5½- or 6-quart slow cooker, combine mushrooms and pearl onions. Stir in ½ cup broth, the wine, tomato paste, garlic salt, rosemary, thyme, pepper, and bay leaf. Add chicken legs to cooker.

2 Cover and cook on low-heat setting for 7 to 8 hours or on high-heat setting for 3½ to 4 hours.

3 Using a slotted spoon, transfer chicken and vegetables to a serving platter. Discard bay leaf. Cover chicken and vegetables and keep warm.

4 For sauce, skim fat from cooking liquid. Measure 2 cups of the cooking liquid, adding additional chicken broth, if necessary, to equal 2 cups total liquid. Transfer liquid to a medium saucepan. In a small bowl, stir the remaining ¼ cup broth into the flour; stir into liquid in saucepan. Cook and stir until thickened and bubbly; cook and stir for 1 minute more. Spoon some of the sauce over chicken. Pass remaining sauce. If desired, serve with mashed potatoes and garnish with parsley.

Nutrition facts per serving: 304 cal., 9 g total fat (2 g sat. fat), 159 mg chol., 548 mg sodium, 9 g carbo., 1 g fiber, 43 g pro.

fennel AND PEAR CHICKEN THIGHS

Prep: 20 minutes
Cook: 7 to 8 hours (low) or
3½ to 4 hours (high)
Makes: 6 servings

- **1 medium fennel bulb, trimmed and cut into ½-inch-thick wedges**
- **2 6- to 7-ounce jars (drained weight) sliced mushrooms, drained**
- **½ cup coarsely snipped dried pears**
- **2 tablespoons quick-cooking tapioca, finely ground**
- **2½ pounds skinless, boneless chicken thighs**
- **¾ teaspoon salt**
- **½ teaspoon dried thyme, crushed**
- **½ teaspoon cracked black pepper**
- **1 cup pear nectar or apple juice**
- **Hot cooked couscous or rice**
- **Fennel tops (optional)**

1 In a 3½- or 4-quart slow cooker, combine sliced fennel, mushrooms, and dried pears. Sprinkle with tapioca. Add chicken thighs; sprinkle with salt, thyme, and pepper. Pour pear nectar over mixture in cooker.

2 Cover and cook on low-heat setting for 7 to 8 hours or on high-heat setting for 3½ to 4 hours. Serve chicken mixture with hot cooked couscous. If desired, garnish with fennel tops.

Nutrition facts per serving: 407 cal., 7 g total fat (2 g sat. fat), 157 mg chol., 657 mg sodium, 41 g carbo., 4 g fiber, 42 g pro.

chicken WITH CREAMY CHIVE SAUCE

Italian salad dressing mix, golden mushroom soup, wine, and flavored cream cheese create this flavorful chicken dish. If you like, serve over pasta or rice with a generous portion of sauce.

Prep: 15 minutes
Cook: 4 to 5 hours (low)
Makes: 6 servings

- **6 skinless, boneless chicken breast halves (about 1½ pounds total)**
- **¼ cup butter**
- **1 0.7-ounce package Italian salad dressing mix**
- **1 10.75-ounce can condensed golden mushroom soup**
- **½ cup dry white wine**
- **½ of an 8-ounce tub cream cheese with chives and onion**
- **Snipped fresh chives (optional)**

1 Place chicken in a 3½- or 4-quart slow cooker. In a medium saucepan, melt the butter. Stir in the dry Italian salad dressing mix. Add mushroom soup, wine, and cream cheese, stirring until combined. Pour over the chicken.

2 Cover and cook on low-heat setting for 4 to 5 hours. Serve chicken with sauce. If desired, sprinkle with fresh chives.

Nutrition facts per serving: 310 cal., 17 g total fat (9 g sat. fat), 110 mg chol., 1,043 mg sodium, 6 g carbo., 0 g fiber, 28 g pro.

chicken STROGANOFF

For an easy dinner party, serve this elegant dish with your favorite steamed vegetables, purchased dinner rolls, and an extra-special dessert from the bakery.

Prep: 20 minutes
Cook: 6 to 7 hours (low) or
      3 to 3½ hours (high)
Makes: 6 to 8 servings

- 2 **pounds skinless, boneless chicken breast halves and/or thighs**
- 1 **cup chopped onion**
- 1 **4-ounce can (drained weight) sliced mushrooms, drained**
- 2 **10.75-ounce cans condensed cream of mushroom soup with roasted garlic**
- ⅓ **cup water**
- 12 **ounces dried wide egg noodles**
- 1 **8-ounce carton dairy sour cream**
  Freshly ground black pepper (optional)
  Fresh thyme sprigs (optional)

1 Cut chicken into 1-inch pieces. In a 3½- or 4-quart slow cooker, combine chicken pieces, onion, and mushrooms. In a medium bowl, stir together mushroom soup and the water. Pour over chicken and vegetables.

2 Cover and cook on low-heat setting for 6 to 7 hours or on high-heat setting for 3 to 3½ hours.

3 Cook noodles according to package directions; drain well. Just before serving, stir sour cream into mixture in cooker. Serve over hot cooked noodles. If desired, sprinkle with pepper and garnish with thyme.

Nutrition facts per serving: 539 cal., 14 g total fat (6 g sat. fat), 156 mg chol., 850 mg sodium, 55 g carbo., 3 g fiber, 57 g pro.

sweet AND SMOKY CHICKEN

Wondering what to do with the extra chipotle chile peppers? Pack them in a freezer container covered with the sauce from the can. Then seal, label, and freeze the chiles for up to 2 months. Thaw them in the refrigerator when you need them.

Prep: 15 minutes
Cook: 6 to 7 hours (low) or
        3 to 3½ hours (high)
Makes: 4 to 6 servings

2½ to 3 pounds meaty chicken pieces (breast halves, thighs, and drumsticks), skinned

¼ teaspoon salt

⅛ teaspoon ground black pepper

1 cup chicken broth

½ cup seedless raspberry jam

½ cup snipped dried apricots

1 to 2 canned chipotle chile peppers in adobo sauce, chopped, plus 1 tablespoon adobo sauce (see tip, page 25)

1 tablespoon quick-cooking tapioca, finely ground

1 Place chicken in a 3½- or 4-quart slow cooker. Sprinkle with salt and black pepper. For sauce, in a small bowl, stir together broth, raspberry jam, dried apricots, chile peppers and adobo sauce, and tapioca. Pour over chicken in cooker.

2 Cover and cook on low-heat setting for 6 to 7 hours or on high-heat setting for 3 to 3½ hours.

3 Transfer chicken to a serving platter. Serve sauce over chicken.

Nutrition facts per serving: 412 cal., 10 g total fat (3 g sat. fat), 115 mg chol., 549 mg sodium, 41 g carbo., 2 g fiber, 38 g pro.

finger LICKIN' BARBECUE CHICKEN

This recipe's secrets come from unexpected sources: the hot dog stand (mustard) and the breakfast table (preserves).

Prep: 10 minutes
Cook: 6 to 8 hours (low) or 3 to 4 hours (high)
Makes: 4 to 6 servings

2½ to 3 pounds chicken drumsticks, skinned if desired

1 cup bottled barbecue sauce

⅓ cup apricot or peach preserves

2 teaspoons yellow mustard

1 Place chicken in a 3½- or 4-quart slow cooker. In a small bowl, stir together the barbecue sauce, preserves, and mustard. Pour over chicken in cooker.

2 Cover and cook on low-heat setting for 6 to 8 hours or on high-heat setting for 3 to 4 hours. Remove chicken to serving dish; cover and keep warm. If desired, transfer sauce mixture in cooker to a medium saucepan. Bring to boiling; reduce heat. Simmer, uncovered, for 10 minutes or until desired consistency. Serve sauce with chicken.

Nutrition facts per serving: 456 cal., 17 g total fat (4 g sat. fat), 154 mg chol., 963 mg sodium, 37 g carbo., 2 g fiber, 38 g pro.

mole WITH CHICKEN AND RICE

In this chicken favorite, mole, a spicy sauce made with chiles and chocolate, is a treat for the taste buds.

Prep: 25 minutes
Cook: 9 to 11 hours (low) or
 4½ to 5½ hours (high)
Makes: 4 to 6 servings

- 1 **14.5-ounce can diced tomatoes, undrained**
- ½ **cup chopped onion**
- ¼ **cup slivered almonds, toasted**
- 3 **cloves garlic, quartered**
- 2 **canned jalapeño chile peppers, drained (see tip, page 25)**
- 3 **tablespoons unsweetened cocoa powder**
- 3 **tablespoons raisins**
- 1 **tablespoon sesame seeds**
- 1 **teaspoon sugar**
- ¼ **teaspoon salt**
- ¼ **teaspoon ground cinnamon**
- ⅛ **teaspoon ground nutmeg**
- ⅛ **teaspoon ground coriander**
- 2 **tablespoons quick-cooking tapioca**
- 1 **2½- to 3-pound broiler-fryer chicken, cut up and skinned**
- 2 **tablespoons slivered almonds, toasted**
  Hot cooked rice

1 For mole, in a blender or food processor, combine undrained tomatoes, onion, the ¼ cup almonds, the garlic, chile peppers, cocoa powder, raisins, sesame seeds, sugar, salt, cinnamon, nutmeg, and coriander. Cover; blend or process until mixture is a coarse puree.

2 Place tapioca in a 3½- or 4-quart slow cooker. Add chicken; pour mole over chicken.

3 Cover and cook on low-heat setting for 9 to 11 hours or on high-heat setting for 4½ to 5½ hours.

4 Transfer chicken to a serving platter. Stir the sauce; pour sauce over chicken. Sprinkle with the 2 tablespoons almonds. Serve with hot cooked rice.

Nutrition facts per serving: 448 cal., 23 g total fat (5 g sat. fat), 99 mg chol., 586 mg sodium, 24 g carbo., 4 g fiber, 36 g pro.

green CHILE TACO SALAD

Any leftover mixture can be used to make nachos another day.

Prep: 15 minutes
Cook: 6 to 8 hours (low) or
          3 to 3½ hours (high)
Makes: 6 servings

- 1 pound ground turkey or chicken or lean ground beef
- 1 large onion, finely chopped
- 1 large green sweet pepper, chopped
- 1 16-ounce jar mild green salsa
- 1 15- to 16-ounce can Great Northern beans, rinsed and drained
- 1 10-ounce bag romaine salad mix
- 3 cups crushed tortilla chips
- ½ cup sliced green onions
- ½ cup chopped fresh cilantro
  Chopped tomato (optional)

1 In a large skillet, brown ground meat; drain fat. Transfer to a 3½- to 4-quart slow cooker. Stir in onion, sweet pepper, salsa, and beans.

2 Cover and cook on low-heat setting for 6 to 8 hours or on high-heat setting for 3 to 3½ hours.

3 Divide greens among 6 plates. Top with salsa mixture. Sprinkle with chips, green onions, and cilantro. If desired, top with chopped tomato.

Nutrition facts per serving: 375 cal., 13 g total fat (2 g sat. fat), 60 mg chol., 475 mg sodium, 44 g carbo., 9 g fiber, 22 g pro.

teriyaki AND ORANGE CHICKEN

Here's a sauce that's sweet and full of flavor. Use orange sections or slices to garnish the meal.

Prep: 15 minutes
Cook: 4 to 5 hours (low) or
2 to 2½ hours (high)
Makes: 4 servings

- 1 **16-ounce package frozen loose-pack broccoli, carrots, and water chestnuts**
- 2 **tablespoons quick-cooking tapioca**
- 1 **pound skinless, boneless chicken breast halves or thighs, cut into 1-inch pieces**
- ¾ **cup chicken broth**
- 3 **tablespoons orange marmalade**
- 2 **tablespoons bottled teriyaki sauce**
- 1 **teaspoon dry mustard**
- ½ **teaspoon ground ginger**
- 2 **cups hot cooked brown rice**

1 In a 3½- or 4-quart slow cooker, combine frozen vegetables and tapioca. Add chicken.

2 In a small bowl, combine chicken broth, orange marmalade, teriyaki sauce, dry mustard, and ginger. Pour over mixture in cooker.

3 Cover and cook on low-heat setting for 4 to 5 hours or on high-heat setting for 2 to 2½ hours. Serve with hot cooked rice.

Nutrition facts per serving: 375 cal., 4 g total fat (1 g sat. fat), 79 mg chol., 790 mg sodium, 52 g carbo., 4 g fiber, 30 g pro.

chicken JAMBALAYA

The spicy Cajun flavor of this slow-cooked Louisiana favorite will put a zip in your day.

Prep: 15 minutes
Cook: 5 to 6 hours (low) or
2½ to 3 hours (high),
+ 45 minutes on high
Makes: 6 servings

- **8 ounces skinless, boneless chicken breast halves**
- **1 16-ounce package frozen (yellow, green, and red) peppers and onion stir-fry vegetables**
- **8 ounces smoked turkey sausage, halved lengthwise and cut into ½-inch-thick slices**
- **2 cups water**
- **1 14.5-ounce can diced tomatoes with jalapeño chile peppers, undrained**
- **1 8-ounce package jambalaya rice mix**

1 Cut chicken into ½-inch strips. Place frozen vegetables in a 3½- or 4-quart slow cooker. Top with chicken strips and turkey sausage slices. Add the water, undrained tomatoes, and, if present, seasoning packet from rice. Set dry rice mix aside.

2 Cover and cook on low-heat setting for 5 to 6 hours or on high-heat setting for 2½ to 3 hours.

3 Stir in dry rice mix. If using low-heat setting, turn to high-heat setting. Cover and cook for about 45 minutes more or until most of the liquid is absorbed and rice is tender.

Nutrition facts per serving: 265 cal., 4 g total fat (1 g sat. fat), 47 mg chol., 1,118 mg sodium, 37 g carbo., 2 g fiber, 19 g pro.

mu SHU–STYLE CHICKEN

This slow-cooker version of mu shu differs from the classic because it features chicken instead of pork and is served in tortillas instead of thin pancakes.

Prep: 20 minutes
Cook: 6 to 7 hours (low) or
      3 to 3½ hours (high)
Makes: 4 servings

2½ **to 3 pounds meaty chicken
    pieces (breast halves, thighs,
    and drumsticks), skinned**
 ¼ **teaspoon salt**
 ⅛ **teaspoon ground black pepper**
 ½ **cup water**
 ¼ **cup soy sauce**
 2 **teaspoons toasted sesame oil**
 ¾ **teaspoon ground ginger**
 8 **7- to 8-inch flour tortillas**
 ½ **cup bottled hoisin sauce**
 2 **cups packaged shredded
    broccoli (broccoli slaw mix)
    or packaged shredded
    cabbage with carrot
    (coleslaw mix)**

1 Place chicken pieces in a 3½- or 4-quart slow cooker. Sprinkle with salt and pepper. In a small bowl, stir together the water, soy sauce, sesame oil, and ginger. Pour over chicken in cooker.

2 Cover and cook on low-heat setting for 6 to 7 hours or on high-heat setting for 3 to 3½ hours.

3 Remove chicken, reserving cooking liquid. When cool enough to handle, remove chicken from bones; discard bones. Using two forks, pull chicken apart into shreds. Return chicken to cooker; heat through.

4 To serve, spread each tortilla with 1 tablespoon of the hoisin sauce. Using a slotted spoon, spoon shredded chicken just below centers of tortillas. Top with shredded broccoli. Fold bottom edge of each tortilla up and over filling. Fold in opposite sides; roll up from bottom.

Nutrition facts per serving: 520 cal., 18 g total fat (4 g sat. fat), 115 mg chol., 1,315 mg sodium, 44 g carbo., 3 g fiber, 44 g pro.

brunswick STEW

Early Virginia settlers made this hearty stew with squirrel meat. Our updated version simmers all day in your slow cooker and features chicken and ham.

Prep: 20 minutes
Cook: 8 to 10 hours (low) or
    4 to 5 hours (high);
    + 45 minutes on high
Makes: 6 servings

- 3 **medium onions, cut into thin wedges**
- 2 **pounds meaty chicken pieces (breasts, thighs, and drumsticks), skinned**
- 1½ **cups diced cooked ham (8 ounces)**
- 1 **14.5-ounce can diced tomatoes, undrained**
- 1 **14-ounce can chicken broth**
- 4 **cloves garlic, minced**
- 1 **tablespoon Worcestershire sauce**
- 1 **teaspoon dry mustard**
- 1 **teaspoon dried thyme, crushed**
- ¼ **teaspoon ground black pepper**
- ¼ **teaspoon bottled hot pepper sauce**
- 1 **10-ounce package frozen sliced okra**
- 1 **cup frozen baby lima beans**
- 1 **cup frozen whole kernel corn**

1 Place onions in a 3½- to 4-quart slow cooker. Top with chicken and ham. In a small bowl, combine undrained tomatoes, broth, garlic, Worcestershire sauce, dry mustard, thyme, pepper, and hot pepper sauce; pour over chicken and ham.

2 Cover and cook on low-heat setting for 8 to 10 hours or on high-heat setting for 4 to 5 hours.

3 If desired, remove chicken; cool slightly. (Keep lid on the slow cooker.) Remove meat from chicken bones; cut meat into bite-size pieces. Return chicken to cooker; discard bones.

4 Add okra, lima beans, and corn to cooker. If using low-heat setting, turn to high-heat setting. Cover and cook for 45 minutes more or until vegetables are tender.

Nutrition facts per serving: 417 cal., 11 g total fat (3 g sat. fat), 124 mg chol., 1,252 mg sodium, 36 g carbo., 7 g fiber, 43 g pro.

turkey CHABLIS

Only wines grown in the village of Chablis, France, are truly Chablis wines. But did you know that the grape used in these wines is Chardonnay? You can use a Chardonnay in this recipe or your favorite dry white wine.

Prep: 15 minutes
Cook: 9 to 10 hours (low) or
        4½ to 5 hours (high)
Makes: 6 to 8 servings

- ¾ **cup dry white wine**
- ½ **cup chopped onion**
- 1 **bay leaf**
- 1 **clove garlic, minced**
- 1 **3½- to 4-pound frozen boneless turkey, thawed**
- 1 **teaspoon dried rosemary, crushed**
- ¼ **teaspoon ground black pepper**
- ⅓ **cup half-and-half, light cream, or milk**
- 2 **tablespoons cornstarch**

1 In a 3½- to 6-quart slow cooker, combine wine, onion, bay leaf, and garlic. Remove netting from turkey, if present. Remove gravy packet, if present, and chill for another use. In a small bowl, combine rosemary and pepper. Sprinkle rosemary mixture evenly over turkey; rub in with your fingers. Place turkey in cooker.

2 Cover and cook on low-heat setting for 9 to 10 hours or on high-heat setting for 4½ to 5 hours. Remove turkey from cooker, reserving juices. Cover turkey and keep warm.

3 For gravy, strain juices into a glass measuring cup; skim off fat. Measure 1⅓ cups juices. Pour juices into a small saucepan. Combine half-and-half and cornstarch; stir into juices in saucepan. Cook and stir over medium heat until thickened and bubbly. Cook and stir for 2 minutes more.

4 Slice turkey; arrange on a serving platter. Spoon some of the gravy over turkey. Pass remaining gravy.

Nutrition facts per serving: 365 cal., 9 g total fat (3 g sat. fat), 176 mg chol., 193 mg sodium, 5 g carbo., 0 g fiber, 58 g pro.

sesame-ginger TURKEY WRAPS

If you're not feeding a crowd, refrigerate or freeze the leftover turkey to reheat for another meal.

Prep: 20 minutes
Cook: 6 to 7 hours (low) or
3 to 3½ hours (high)
Stand: 5 minutes
Makes: 12 servings

   Nonstick cooking spray
3 turkey thighs, skinned
(3½ to 4 pounds total)
1 cup bottled sesame-ginger
stir-fry sauce
¼ cup water
1 16-ounce package shredded
broccoli (broccoli slaw mix)
12 8-inch flour tortillas,
warmed*
¾ cup sliced green onions

1 Lightly coat a 3½- or 4-quart slow cooker with cooking spray. Place turkey thighs in prepared cooker. In a small bowl, stir together stir-fry sauce and the water. Pour over turkey in cooker.

2 Cover and cook on low-heat setting for 6 to 7 hours or on high-heat setting for 3 to 3½ hours.

3 Remove turkey from cooker; cool slightly. Remove turkey from bones; discard bones. Using two forks, shred turkey into bite-size pieces. Return to mixture in cooker. Place broccoli slaw mix in sauce mixture in the cooker. Stir to coat; cover and let stand for 5 minutes. Using a slotted spoon, remove turkey and broccoli from cooker.

4 To assemble, place some of the turkey mixture on each warmed tortilla. Top turkey mixture with green onions. If desired, spoon some of the sauce from cooker on top of green onions. Roll up and serve immediately.

***Note:** To warm tortillas, preheat oven to 350°F. Stack tortillas and wrap tightly in foil. Heat in the oven for about 10 minutes or until heated through.

Nutrition facts per serving: 207 cal., 5 g total fat (1 g sat. fat), 67 mg chol., 422 mg sodium, 20 g carbo., 2 g fiber, 20 g pro.

turkey AND PASTA PRIMAVERA

A sprinkling of Parmesan cheese brings a tantalizing accent to a creamy blend of turkey, pasta, and veggies.

Prep: 15 minutes
Cook: 4 to 5 hours (low) or 2 to
　　　2½ hours (high)
Makes: 8 servings

2　pounds turkey breast
　　tenderloins or skinless,
　　boneless chicken breast
　　halves, cut into 1-inch pieces

1　16-ounce package frozen
　　loose-pack stir-fry
　　vegetables (sugar snap
　　peas, carrots, onions, and
　　mushrooms)

2　teaspoons dried basil,
　　oregano, or Italian
　　seasoning, crushed

1　16-ounce jar Alfredo pasta
　　sauce

12　ounces dried linguine or
　　spaghetti, broken

　　Shredded Parmesan cheese
　　(optional)

1 In a 4½- to 6-quart slow cooker, combine turkey and frozen vegetables. Sprinkle with dried herb. Stir in Alfredo sauce.

2 Cover and cook on low-heat setting for 4 to 5 hours or on high-heat setting for 2 to 2½ hours.

3 Cook pasta according to package directions; drain. Stir pasta into mixture in slow cooker. If desired, sprinkle individual servings with Parmesan cheese.

Nutrition facts per serving: 488 cal., 19 g total fat (0 g sat. fat), 99 mg chol., 267 mg sodium, 39 g carbo., 3 g fiber, 37 g pro.

Two for One

Many slow-cooker main dishes make enough servings that you will have enough for another meal. Cool the leftovers slightly and transfer them to a freezer container. Label and freeze them for up to 6 months.

To serve, thaw the leftovers in the refrigerator and reheat them on the stove top or in a microwave oven, stirring several times.

effortless
SOUPS AND STEWS

Creamy Tortellini Soup, *recipe page 162*

italian VEGETABLE SOUP

A spoonful of pesto and a sprinkling of Parmesan cheese are optional additions to the final bowl of soup, but they definitely add a crowning touch.

Prep: 20 minutes
Cook: 6 to 8 hours (low) or
3 to 4 hours (high)
Makes: 6 to 8 side-dish
servings

1 **9-ounce package frozen cut green beans**

½ **of a 16-ounce package frozen cauliflower**

1 **14.5-ounce can diced tomatoes with basil, garlic, and oregano, undrained**

½ **cup chopped onion (1 medium)**

½ **cup sliced celery (1 stalk)**

¼ **cup regular barley (not quick-cooking)**

1 **clove garlic, minced**

¼ **teaspoon ground black pepper**

3 **cups reduced-sodium chicken broth**

1½ **cups reduced-sodium vegetable juice**

¼ **cup purchased basil pesto (optional)**

Finely shredded Parmesan cheese (optional)

1 In a 3½- or 4-quart slow cooker, combine green beans, cauliflower, tomatoes, onion, celery, barley, garlic, and pepper. Pour broth and vegetable juice over mixture in cooker.

2 Cover and cook on low-heat setting for 6 to 8 hours or on high-heat setting for 3 to 4 hours. If desired, top each serving with pesto and Parmesan cheese.

Nutrition facts per serving: 81 cal., 0 g total fat (0 g sat. fat), 0 mg chol., 520 mg sodium, 17 g carbo., 3 g fiber, 4 g pro.

french COUNTRY SOUP

Crusty pieces of French bread are perfect for soaking up the wonderful rosemary-seasoned broth in this bean-and-beef combo.

Prep: 20 minutes
Stand: 1 hour
Cook: 8 to 10 hours (low) or
      4 to 5 hours (high)
Makes: 6 servings

- 8 ounces dry navy, Great Northern, or white kidney (cannellini) beans
- 6 cups water
- 1 pound beef or lamb stew meat, cut into 1-inch cubes
- 4 cups reduced-sodium chicken broth
- 2 medium carrots, cut into 1-inch pieces
- 2 stalks celery, cut into 1-inch pieces
- 1 large onion, cut into wedges
- 1 cup dry white wine
- 6 cloves garlic, minced
- 3 bay leaves
- 1½ teaspoons dried rosemary, crushed
- ½ teaspoon salt
- ¼ teaspoon ground black pepper

1 Rinse and drain beans. In a 4-quart Dutch oven, combine beans and the water. Bring to boiling; reduce heat. Simmer for 10 minutes. Remove from heat. Cover and let stand for 1 hour.

2 Drain beans in colander; rinse beans. In a 3½- to 6-quart slow cooker, combine beans, meat, broth, carrots, celery, onion, wine, garlic, bay leaves, rosemary, salt, and pepper.

3 Cover and cook on low-heat setting for 8 to 10 hours or on high-heat setting for 4 to 5 hours. Discard bay leaves.

Nutrition facts per serving: 315 cal., 4 g total fat (1 g sat. fat), 45 mg chol., 694 mg sodium, 37 g carbo., 12 g fiber, 28 g pro.

beef-vegetable SOUP

On a super-busy day, start this soup simmering before leaving home and it will be ready to serve when dinnertime rolls around.

Prep: 25 minutes
Cook: 8 to 10 hours (low) or
4 to 5 hours (high)
Makes: 4 or 5 servings

1 **pound boneless beef chuck roast, cut into 1-inch pieces**

1 **tablespoon cooking oil**

2 **14½-ounce cans diced tomatoes, undrained**

1 **cup water**

3 **medium carrots, sliced**

2 **small potatoes, peeled if desired, cut into ½-inch cubes**

1 **cup chopped onion**

1 **teaspoon salt**

½ **teaspoon dried thyme, crushed**

½ **cup frozen loose-pack peas, thawed**

1 In a large skillet, brown meat in oil over medium-high heat.

2 Transfer meat to a 3½- to 4½-quart slow cooker. Add undrained tomatoes, the water, carrots, potatoes, onion, salt, and thyme to cooker.

3 Cover and cook on low-heat setting for 8 to 10 hours or on high-heat setting for 4 or 5 hours. Stir in peas.

Nutrition facts per serving: 335 cal., 8 g total fat (2 g sat. fat), 67 mg chol., 1,054 mg sodium, 35 g carbo., 5 g fiber, 29 g pro.

chicken TORTILLA SOUP

There's no need to measure lots of herbs or spices for this soup. They're already in the chicken broth and Mexican-style tomatoes.

Prep: 15 minutes
Cook: 6 to 7 hours (low) or
3 to 3½ hours (high)
Makes: 4 servings

2   **14-ounce cans chicken broth
with roasted garlic**

1   **14.5-ounce can Mexican-style
stewed tomatoes, undrained**

2   **cups shredded cooked
chicken (about 10 ounces)**

2   **cups frozen (yellow, green,
and red) sweet peppers and
onion stir-fry vegetables**

1   **cup tortilla chips**

   **Sliced fresh jalapeño chile
peppers (optional; see tip,
page 25)**

1 In a 3½- or 4-quart slow cooker, combine broth, undrained tomatoes, chicken, and frozen vegetables.

2 Cover and cook on low-heat setting for 6 to 7 hours or on high-heat setting for 3 to 3½ hours.

3 To serve, ladle soup into warm soup bowls and top with tortilla chips. If desired, top with chile peppers.

Nutrition facts per serving: 181 cal., 4 g total fat (1 g sat. fat), 36 mg chol., 1,383 mg sodium, 19 g carbo., 1 g fiber, 18 g pro.

chicken AND VEGETABLE BEAN SOUP

When there's no leftover cooked chicken in the fridge, pick up a roasted bird at your supermarket's deli section.

Prep: 15 minutes
Stand: 1 hour
Cook: 8 to 10 hours (low) or
4 to 5 hours (high),
+ 30 minutes on high
Makes: 4 to 6 servings

1 **cup dry Great Northern beans**

6 **cups water**

1 **cup chopped onion**

1 **medium fennel bulb, trimmed and cut into ½-inch pieces**

2 **medium carrots, chopped**

2 **cloves garlic, minced**

2 **tablespoons snipped fresh parsley**

1 **teaspoon dried rosemary, crushed**

¼ **teaspoon ground black pepper**

4½ **cups chicken broth**

2½ **cups shredded or chopped cooked chicken**

1 **14.5-ounce can diced tomatoes, undrained**

1 Rinse beans; drain. In a large saucepan, combine beans and the water. Bring to boiling; reduce heat. Simmer, uncovered, for 10 minutes. Remove from heat. Cover and let stand for 1 hour. Drain and rinse beans.

2 Meanwhile, in a 3½- to 5-quart slow cooker, combine onion, fennel, carrots, garlic, parsley, rosemary, and pepper. Place beans on top of vegetables in cooker. Pour broth over all.

3 Cover and cook on low-heat setting for 8 to 10 hours or on high-heat setting for 4 to 5 hours.

4 If using low-heat setting, turn to high-heat setting. Stir in chicken and undrained tomatoes. Cover and cook for about 30 minutes more or until heated through.

Nutrition facts per serving: 426 cal., 10 g total fat (3 g sat. fat), 78 mg chol., 1,454 mg sodium, 46 g carbo., 15 g fiber, 40 g pro.

savory BEAN AND SPINACH SOUP

Just like Goldilocks, you'll find the converted rice is "just right." Long-grain or quick-cooking rice would be "too soft" for the long-cooking soup.

Prep: 15 minutes
Cook: 5 to 7 hours (low) or
2½ to 3½ hours (high)
Makes: 6 servings

3   **14-ounce cans vegetable broth**

1   **15-ounce can tomato puree**

1   **15-ounce can white or Great Northern beans, rinsed and drained**

½   **cup converted rice**

½   **cup finely chopped onion**

2   **cloves garlic, minced**

1   **teaspoon dried basil, crushed**

¼   **teaspoon salt**

¼   **teaspoon ground black pepper**

8   **cups coarsely chopped fresh spinach or kale leaves**

   Finely shredded Parmesan cheese

1 In a 3½- or 4-quart slow cooker, combine broth, tomato puree, beans, rice, onion, garlic, basil, salt, and pepper.

2 Cover and cook on low-heat setting for 5 to 7 hours or on high-heat setting for 2½ to 3½ hours.

3 Stir spinach into soup. Serve with Parmesan cheese.

Nutrition facts per serving: 150 cal., 3 g total fat (1 g sat. fat), 4 mg chol., 1,137 mg sodium, 31 g carbo., 8 g fiber, 9 g pro.

rich BEEF AND BARLEY SOUP

Vary the character of this hearty beef soup by the type of spaghetti sauce you choose. One time try a sauce with lots garlic or mushrooms, and another time use an herb-seasoned sauce.

Prep: 30 minutes
Cook: 9 to 10 hours (low) or
4½ to 5 hours (high)
Makes: 6 to 8 servings

1½ **pounds beef stew meat**

1 **tablespoon cooking oil**

1 **cup thinly sliced carrot**

1 **cup sliced celery**

1 **medium onion, thinly sliced**

½ **cup coarsely chopped green
sweet pepper**

4 **cups beef broth**

1 **14.5-ounce can tomatoes,
undrained, cut up**

1 **cup purchased spaghetti
sauce**

⅔ **cup pearl barley**

1½ **teaspoons dried basil,
crushed**

½ **teaspoon salt**

¼ **teaspoon ground black
pepper**

¼ **cup snipped fresh parsley**

1 Cut meat into 1-inch pieces. In a large skillet, brown meat, half at a time, in oil over medium-high heat. Drain well.

2 Meanwhile, in a 3½- to 6-quart slow cooker, combine carrot, celery, onion, and sweet pepper. Add broth, undrained tomatoes, spaghetti sauce, barley, basil, salt, and pepper. Stir in browned meat.

3 Cover and cook on low-heat setting for 9 to 10 hours or on high-heat setting for 4½ to 5 hours. Skim off fat. Stir in parsley.

Nutrition facts per serving: 408 cal., 19 g total fat (7 g sat. fat), 72 mg chol., 998 mg sodium, 30 g carbo., 6 g fiber, 29 g pro.

smoked SAUSAGE-LENTIL SOUP

Prep: 25 minutes
Cook: 6 to 7 hours (low) or
   3 to 3½ hours (high)
Makes: 6 servings

1 small fennel bulb

6 cups water

6 ounces smoked sausage, cut
   into ½-inch pieces

1¼ cups dry brown lentils, rinsed
   and drained

2 carrots, chopped

1 medium onion, chopped

4 cloves garlic, minced

1 teaspoon kosher or sea salt
   or ¾ teaspoon regular salt

¼ teaspoon freshly ground
   black pepper

2 tablespoons red wine vinegar

   Kosher salt, sea salt, or
   regular salt

   Freshly ground black pepper

1 Remove fennel tops and reserve for garnish. Chop enough of the fennel bulb to equal 1 cup.

2 In a 3½- to 5-quart slow cooker, combine fennel, the water, sausage, lentils, carrots, onion, garlic, the salt, and the ¼ teaspoon pepper.

3 Cover and cook on low-heat setting for 6 to 7 hours or on high-heat setting for 3 to 3½ hours.

4 Before serving, stir in vinegar. Season to taste with additional salt and pepper. Garnish with reserved fennel tops.

Nutrition facts per serving: 273 cal., 10 g total fat (3 g sat. fat), 19 mg chol., 776 mg sodium, 30 g carbo., 13 g fiber, 17 g pro.

wild RICE AND CHICKEN SOUP

Prep: 20 minutes
Cook: 6 to 8 hours (low) or
  3 to 4 hours (high)
Makes: 8 to 10 servings

2½ **cups chopped cooked chicken
  (about 12 ounces)**

2 **cups sliced fresh mushrooms**

2 **medium carrots, coarsely
  shredded**

2 **stalks celery, sliced**

1 **10¾-ounce can condensed
  cream of chicken or cream of
  mushroom soup**

1 **6-ounce package long-grain
  and wild rice mix**

5 **cups chicken broth**

5 **cups water**

1 In a 5- to 6-quart slow cooker, combine cooked chicken, mushrooms, carrots, celery, soup, uncooked rice, and the contents of the rice seasoning packet. Gradually stir in chicken broth and the water.

2 Cover and cook on low-heat setting for 6 to 8 hours or on high-heat setting for 3 to 4 hours.

Nutrition facts per serving: 221 cal., 7 g total fat (2 g sat. fat), 44 mg chol., 1,251 mg sodium, 23 g carbo., 2 g fiber, 18 g pro.

chicken CHILI

Does your supermarket bakery carry bread bowls? If it does, they are ideal for serving this awesome chili.

Prep: 25 minutes
Cook: 5 to 6 hours (low) or
    2½ to 3 hours (high)
Makes: 2 servings

Nonstick cooking spray

8 **ounces skinless, boneless chicken breast halves, cut into 1-inch pieces**

1 **15-ounce can white kidney (cannellini) or Great Northern beans, rinsed and drained**

1¼ **cups reduced-sodium chicken broth**

¼ **cup chopped onion**

⅓ **cup chopped green sweet pepper**

½ **of a small fresh jalapeño chile pepper, seeded and finely chopped (see tip, page 25)**

¼ **teaspoon ground cumin**

¼ **teaspoon dried oregano, crushed**

⅛ **teaspoon ground white pepper**

1 **clove garlic, minced**

2 **tablespoons chopped tomato (optional)**

2 **tablespoons sliced green onion (optional)**

2 **tablespoons shredded Monterey Jack cheese (1 ounce) (optional)**

1 Lightly coat an unheated medium skillet with cooking spray. Preheat skillet over medium-high heat. Brown chicken in hot skillet; drain off fat.

2 In a 1½-quart slow cooker, combine chicken, drained beans, broth, onion, sweet pepper, chile pepper, cumin, oregano, white pepper, and garlic.

3 Cover and cook on low-heat setting for 5 to 6 hours or on high-heat setting for 2½ to 3 hours. If no heat setting is available, cook for 4 to 5 hours.

4 If desired, sprinkle individual servings with tomato, green onion, and cheese.

Nutrition facts per serving: 275 cal., 2 g total fat (0 g sat. fat), 66 mg chol., 750 mg sodium, 33 g carbo., 11 g fiber, 40 g pro.

black BEAN AND KIELBASA SOUP

Round out this hearty sausage-and-bean combo with corn bread sticks or muffins.

Prep: 15 minutes
Cook: 6 to 8 hours (low) or
　　　3 to 4 hours (high)
Makes: 6 servings

2　**19-ounce cans ready-to-serve black bean soup**

1　**14.5-ounce can diced tomatoes with garlic and onion, undrained**

1　**pound cooked smoked Polish sausage, halved lengthwise and cut into ½-inch-thick slices**

1　**cup frozen loose-pack whole kernel corn**

1 In a 3½- to 4½-quart slow cooker, stir together black bean soup, undrained tomatoes, sausage, and corn.

2 Cover and cook on low-heat setting for 6 to 8 hours or on high-heat setting for 3 to 4 hours.

Nutrition facts per serving: 425 cal., 24 g total fat (11 g sat. fat), 55 mg chol., 1,487 mg sodium, 34 g carbo., 8 g fiber, 17 g pro.

smashed POTATO SOUP

Potatoes blend with cheddar cheese, cream, and roasted garlic in this chunky, good-to-the-last-spoonful soup.

Prep: 25 minutes
Cook: 8 to 10 hours (low) or
    4 to 5 hours (high)
Makes: 8 servings

3½ **pounds potatoes, cut into
¾-inch cubes**

½ **cup chopped yellow and/or
red sweet pepper**

1½ **teaspoons bottled roasted
garlic**

½ **teaspoon ground black
pepper**

4½ **cups chicken broth**

½ **cup whipping cream, half-
and-half, or light cream**

1 **cup shredded cheddar cheese
(4 ounces)**

½ **cup thinly sliced green onions**

  Sliced green onions (optional)

1 In a 4- to 6-quart slow cooker, combine potatoes, sweet pepper, garlic, and black pepper. Pour broth over all.

2 Cover and cook on low-heat setting for 8 to 10 hours or on high-heat setting for 4 to 5 hours.

3 Mash potatoes slightly with a potato masher. Stir in whipping cream, cheddar cheese, and the ½ cup green onions. If desired, top individual servings with additional sliced green onions.

Nutrition facts per serving: 243 cal., 11 g total fat (6 g sat. fat), 37 mg chol., 644 mg sodium, 30 g carbo., 3 g fiber, 8 g pro.

creamy TORTELLINI SOUP

White sauce mix and dried tortellini make this satisfying soup extra easy; stirring in the spinach at the last minute gives it fresh-from-the garden flavor.

Prep: 20 minutes
Cook: 5 to 6 hours (low),
       + 1 hour, or 2½ to
       3 hours (high),
       + 45 minutes
Makes: 4 servings

- 1 **1.8-ounce envelope white sauce mix**
- 4 **cups water**
- 1 **14-ounce can vegetable broth**
- 1½ **cups sliced fresh mushrooms**
- ½ **cup chopped onion**
- 3 **cloves garlic, minced**
- ½ **teaspoon dried basil, crushed**
- ¼ **teaspoon salt**
- ¼ **teaspoon dried oregano, crushed**
- ⅛ **teaspoon cayenne pepper**
- 1 **7- to 8-ounce package dried cheese tortellini (about 2 cups)**
- 1 **12-ounce can evaporated milk**
- 6 **cups fresh baby spinach leaves or torn spinach**

   Ground black pepper (optional)

   Finely shredded Parmesan cheese (optional)

1 Place dry white sauce mix in a 3½- or 4-quart slow cooker. Gradually add the water to the white sauce mix, stirring until smooth. Stir in broth, mushrooms, onion, garlic, basil, salt, oregano, and cayenne pepper.

2 Cover and cook on low-heat setting for 5 to 6 hours or on high-heat setting for 2½ to 3 hours.

3 Stir in dried tortellini. Cover and cook on low-heat setting for 1 hour more or high-heat setting for 45 minutes more.

4 Stir in evaporated milk and spinach. If desired, sprinkle individual servings with black pepper and Parmesan cheese.

Nutrition facts per serving: 450 cal., 18 g total fat (7 g sat. fat), 34 mg chol., 1,710 mg sodium, 53 g carbo., 2 g fiber, 22 g pro.

coq AU VIN STEW

Soak up the flavorful broth with chunks of your favorite crusty bread.

Prep: 20 minutes
Cook: 5 to 6 hours (low) or
2½ to 3 hours (high)
Makes: 4 servings

Nonstick cooking spray

3 **pounds chicken thighs,
skinned**

1 **envelope (½ of a 2.2-ounce
package) beefy onion soup
mix**

1½ **cups loose-pack frozen small
whole onions**

2 **cups fresh mushrooms,
quartered**

½ **cup dry red wine**

**Hot cooked mashed potatoes
(optional)**

**Snipped fresh basil or parsley
(optional)**

1 Lightly coat an unheated large skillet with cooking spray. Preheat skillet over medium heat. Cook chicken thighs, several at a time, in the hot skillet until brown; drain off fat. Place chicken thighs in a 3½- or 4-quart slow cooker.

2 Sprinkle chicken thighs with dry soup mix. Add onions and mushrooms. Pour wine over all.

3 Cover and cook on low-heat setting for 5 to 6 hours or on high-heat setting for 2½ to 3 hours. Using a slotted spoon, remove chicken from slow cooker. Use a fork to remove chicken from the bone, shredding it into bite-size pieces. Discard bones. Return chicken to mixture in cooker. If desired, serve with hot mashed potatoes and sprinkle with basil.

Nutrition facts per serving: 305 cal., 8 g total fat (2 g sat. fat), 161 mg chol., 759 mg sodium, 12 g carbo., 2 g fiber, 41 g pro.

three-bean VEGETARIAN CHILI

Prep: 20 minutes
Cook: 6 to 8 hours (low) or
3 to 4 hours (high)
Makes: 4 servings

1 **15-ounce can no-salt-added red kidney beans, rinsed and drained**

1 **15-ounce can small white beans, rinsed and drained**

1 **15-ounce can low-sodium black beans, rinsed and drained**

1 **14.5-ounce can diced tomatoes and green chile peppers, undrained**

1 **cup beer or chicken broth**

3 **tablespoons chocolate-flavored syrup**

1 **tablespoon chili powder**

2 **teaspoons Cajun seasoning**

   Dairy sour cream (optional)

   Shredded cheddar cheese (optional)

1 In a 3½- or 4-quart slow cooker, combine kidney beans, white beans, black beans, undrained tomatoes and green chile peppers, beer, chocolate syrup, chili powder, and Cajun seasoning.

2 Cover and cook on low-heat setting for 6 to 8 hours or on high-heat setting for 3 to 4 hours. If desired, garnish with sour cream and cheese.

Nutrition facts per serving: 308 cal., 1 g total fat (0 g sat. fat), 0 mg chol., 569 mg sodium, 60 g carbo., 21 g fiber, 21 g pro.

sumptuous SIDES

Cauliflower and Broccoli in Swiss Cheese Sauce, *recipe page 176*

cheesy CAULIFLOWER FOR A CROWD

Cheddar cheese pasta sauce makes this cauliflower potluck pleaser oh-so-easy and oh-so-cheesy.

Prep: 20 minutes
Cook: 6 to 7 hours (low) or
3 to 3½ hours (high)
Makes: 10 to 12 servings

8 **cups cauliflower florets**

1 **large onion, thinly sliced**

½ **teaspoon fennel seeds,
crushed**

1 **14- to 16-ounce jar cheddar
cheese pasta sauce**

**Ground black pepper
(optional)**

1 In a 3½- or 4-quart slow cooker, combine cauliflower, onion, and fennel seeds. Pour pasta sauce over all.

2 Cover and cook on low-heat setting for 6 to 7 hours or on high-heat setting for 3 to 3½ hours. Stir gently. If desired, sprinkle with pepper before serving.

Nutrition facts per serving: 59 cal., 6 g total fat (2 g sat. fat), 16 mg chol., 329 mg sodium, 8 g carbo., 2 g fiber, 3 g pro.

saucy GREEN BEANS AND POTATOES

Prep: 20 minutes
Cook: 6 to 8 hours (low) or
3 to 4 hours (high)
Makes: 12 servings

2 **pounds new potatoes, any large ones halved**

1 **pound fresh green beans, trimmed and halved crosswise**

1 **10.75-ounce can condensed cream of celery soup**

¾ **cup water**

¼ **cup Dijon-style mustard**

¾ **teaspoon dried dillweed**

1 Place potatoes and green beans in a 3½- or 4-quart slow cooker. In a medium bowl, combine soup, water, mustard, and dillweed. Pour over vegetables; gently stir to combine.

2 Cover and cook on low-heat setting for 6 to 8 hours or on high-heat setting for 3 to 4 hours. Gently stir before serving.

Nutrition facts per serving: 95 cal., 2 g total fat (1 g sat. fat), 1 mg chol., 313 mg sodium, 17 g carbo., 3 g fiber, 3 g pro.

cauliflower AND BROCCOLI IN SWISS CHEESE SAUCE

Cheesy and delicious, here's a side dish everyone will love. Served simply with beef or pork, it will take center stage. A side of rice will help sop up the sauce.

Prep: 25 minutes
Cook: 6 to 7 hours (low) or
      3 to 3½ hours (high)
Makes: 10 servings

4 **cups broccoli florets***

4 **cups cauliflower florets***

1 **14- to 16-ounce jar Alfredo pasta sauce**

6 **ounces process Swiss cheese, torn (1½ cups)**

1 **cup chopped onion (1 large)**

1 **teaspoon dried thyme, oregano, or basil, crushed**

¼ **teaspoon ground black pepper**

½ **cup ranch-flavor sliced almonds (optional)**

① In a 3½- or 4-quart slow cooker, combine broccoli, cauliflower, pasta sauce, Swiss cheese, onion, thyme, and pepper.

② Cover and cook on low-heat setting for 6 to 7 hours or on high-heat setting for 3 to 3½ hours.

③ Stir gently before serving. If desired, sprinkle with almonds.

*Test Kitchen Tip: If you like, substitute one-and-a-half 16-ounce packages (about 8 cups) frozen broccoli and cauliflower florets for the fresh. Prepare as directed.

Nutrition facts per serving: 177 cal., 12 g total fat (7 g sat. fat), 37 mg chol., 573 mg sodium, 10 g carbo., 2 g fiber, 8 g pro.

vegetable AND GARBANZO CURRY

You'll find coconut milk in the Asian food section of larger supermarkets or at Asian food specialty stores.

Prep: 25 minutes
Cook: 5 to 6 hours (low) or
2½ to 3 hours (high)
Makes: 4 to 6 servings

3 **cups cauliflower florets**

1 **15-ounce can garbanzo beans
    (chickpeas), rinsed and
    drained**

1 **cup loose-pack frozen cut
    green beans**

1 **cup sliced carrot**

½ **cup chopped onion**

1 **14-ounce can vegetable broth**

2 **to 3 teaspoons curry powder**

1 **14-ounce can light coconut
    milk**

¼ **cup shredded fresh basil
    leaves**

1 In a 3½- or 4-quart slow cooker, combine cauliflower, garbanzo beans, frozen green beans, carrot, and onion. Stir in broth and curry powder.

2 Cover and cook on low-heat setting for 5 to 6 hours or on high-heat setting for 2½ to 3 hours. Stir in coconut milk and basil.

Nutrition facts per serving: 219 cal., 7 g total fat (4 g sat. fat), 0 mg chol., 805 mg sodium, 32 g carbo., 9 g fiber, 8 g pro.

saucy SUCCOTASH

Having a cookout? Serve this cheesy medley along with burgers and brats.

Prep: 15 minutes
Cook: 5 to 6 hours (low) or
2½ to 3 hours (high)
Stand: 10 minutes
Makes: 12 servings

1 **16-ounce package frozen whole kernel corn, thawed**

1 **16-ounce package frozen lima beans, thawed**

1 **14.75-ounce can cream-style corn**

1 **cup chopped red sweet pepper**

1 **cup shredded smoked Gouda cheese (4 ounces)**

½ **cup chopped onion**

2 **teaspoons cumin seeds**

¼ **cup water**

1 **8-ounce carton light dairy sour cream**

1 In a 3½- or 4-quart slow cooker, combine whole kernel corn, lima beans, cream-style corn, sweet pepper, cheese, onion, and cumin seeds. Pour the water over all.

2 Cover and cook on low-heat setting for 5 to 6 hours or on high-heat setting for 2½ to 3 hours.

3 Gently stir in sour cream. Let stand for 10 minutes before serving.

Nutrition facts per serving: 158 cal., 4 g total fat (3 g sat. fat), 14 mg chol., 282 mg sodium, 25 g carbo., 4 g fiber, 7 g pro.

balsamic ROOT VEGETABLES

Prep: 15 minutes
Cook: 9 to 11 hours (low) or
4½ to 5½ hours (high)
Makes: 8 servings

3 medium potatoes, peeled and
cut into 1-inch pieces

3 medium parsnips, peeled and
cut into 1-inch pieces

1 16-ounce package peeled
fresh baby carrots

½ of a 16-ounce package
(2 cups) frozen small whole
onions

1 cup chicken broth

¼ cup balsamic vinegar

2 tablespoons brown sugar

¼ teaspoon salt

¼ teaspoon ground black pepper

2 cloves garlic, minced

1 Combine potatoes, parsnips, carrots, onions, broth, vinegar, brown sugar, salt, pepper, and garlic in a 3½- or 4-quart slow cooker.

2 Cover and cook on low-heat setting for 9 to 11 hours or on high-heat setting for 4½ to 5½ hours.

Nutrition facts per serving: 136 cal., 1 g total fat (0 g sat. fat), 0 mg chol., 235 mg sodium, 32 g carbo., 6 g fiber, 3 g pro.

hot GERMAN-STYLE POTATO SALAD

This slow-cooker version of the old-world favorite is ideal for when the whole family gets together. Stirring in the bacon just before serving helps keep it crisp.

Prep: 25 minutes
Cook: 8 to 9 hours (low) or
      4 to 4½ hours (high)
Makes: 8 servings

6 **cups peeled potatoes, cut into ¾-inch cubes**

1 **cup chopped onion**

1 **cup water**

⅔ **cup cider vinegar**

¼ **cup sugar**

2 **tablespoons quick-cooking tapioca**

1 **teaspoon salt**

¼ **teaspoon celery seeds**

¼ **teaspoon ground black pepper**

6 **slices bacon, crisp-cooked, drained, and crumbled**

1 In a 3½- or 4-quart slow cooker, combine potatoes and onion. In a medium bowl, combine the water, vinegar, sugar, tapioca, salt, celery seeds, and pepper; pour over potatoes in cooker.

2 Cover and cook on low-heat setting for 8 to 9 hours or on high-heat setting for 4 to 4½ hours. Stir in bacon.

Nutrition facts per serving: 160 cal., 2 g total fat (1 g sat. fat), 4 mg chol., 374 mg sodium, 32 g carbo., 2 g fiber, 4 g pro.

hash BROWNS WITH GARLIC-MUSHROOM SAUCE

Prep: 15 minutes
Cook: 8 to 9 hours (low) or
    4 to 4½ hours (high)
Makes: 8 to 10 servings

1 **32-ounce package frozen loose-pack diced hash brown potatoes**

2 **cups shredded Swiss cheese (8 ounces)**

2 **4-ounce cans (drained weight) sliced mushrooms, drained**

1 **tablespoon bottled roasted minced garlic**

1 **10.75-ounce can condensed cream of mushroom soup**

¼ **cup water**

1 In a 3½- or 4-quart slow cooker, combine frozen potatoes, cheese, drained mushrooms, and garlic. Add cream of mushroom soup and the water; stir to combine.

2 Cover and cook on low-heat setting for 8 to 9 hours or on high-heat setting for 4 to 4½ hours. Stir gently before serving.

Nutrition facts per serving: 248 cal., 11 g total fat (6 g sat. fat), 26 mg chol., 482 mg sodium, 26 g carbo., 3 g fiber, 12 g pro.

caramelized ONIONS AND POTATOES

Sweet onions are special varieties that are juicier, contain more sugar, and have a less pungent flavor than regular onions.

Prep: 15 minutes
Cook: 6 to 7 hours (low) or
      3 to 3½ hours (high)
Makes: 6 servings

- **2 large sweet onions (such as Vidalia, Maui, or Walla Walla), thinly sliced**
- **1½ pounds tiny new potatoes, halved**
- **¼ cup butter, melted**
- **½ cup beef or chicken broth**
- **3 tablespoons packed brown sugar**
- **½ teaspoon salt**
- **¼ teaspoon ground black pepper**
- **Ground black pepper (optional)**

1 In a 3½- or 4-quart slow cooker, combine onions and potatoes.

2 In a small bowl, combine melted butter, broth, brown sugar, salt, and the ¼ teaspoon pepper. Pour mixture over onions and potatoes in cooker.

3 Cover and cook on low-heat setting for 6 to 7 hours or on high-heat setting for 3 to 3½ hours. Stir gently before serving. Serve with a slotted spoon. If desired, sprinkle with additional pepper.

Nutrition facts per serving: 194 cal., 8 g total fat (5 g sat. fat), 22 mg chol., 356 mg sodium, 28 g carbo., 3 g fiber, 3 g pro.

easy CHEESY POTATOES

Not just ordinary spuds, these hash browns are dressed up with bacon, leeks, and three kinds of cheese.

Prep: 15 minutes
Cook: 5 to 6 hours (low)
Makes: 12 servings

1 **28-ounce package frozen loose-pack diced hash brown potatoes with onion and peppers, thawed**

1 **10.75-ounce can condensed cream of chicken with herbs soup**

1 **cup finely shredded smoked Gouda cheese (4 ounces)**

1 **cup finely shredded provolone cheese (4 ounces)**

1 **8-ounce package cream cheese, cut into cubes**

¾ **cup milk**

¼ **cup sliced leek or thinly sliced green onions**

½ **teaspoon ground black pepper**

4 **slices bacon, crisp-cooked and crumbled**

① In a 3½- or 4-quart slow cooker, combine thawed potatoes, cream of chicken soup, smoked Gouda cheese, provolone cheese, cream cheese, milk, leek, and pepper.

② Cover and cook on low-heat setting for 5 to 6 hours. To serve, sprinkle with bacon.

Nutrition facts per serving: 218 cal., 14 g total fat (8 g sat. fat), 41 mg chol., 564 mg sodium, 16 g carbo., 2 g fiber, 9 g pro.

wild RICE WITH PECANS AND CHERRIES

If you've been invited to a "turkey and all the trimmings" potluck dinner, help out with the trimmings by bringing this elegant rice pilaf.

Prep: 20 minutes
Cook: 5 to 6 hours (low)
Stand: 10 minutes
Makes: 15 servings

3   14-ounce cans chicken broth

2½   cups wild rice, rinsed and drained

1   cup coarsely shredded carrot

1   4.5-ounce jar (drained weight) sliced mushrooms, drained

2   tablespoons butter or margarine, melted

2   teaspoons dried marjoram, crushed

¼   teaspoon salt

¼   teaspoon ground black pepper

⅔   cup dried tart cherries

⅔   cup chopped green onions

½   cup coarsely chopped pecans, toasted

    Chopped green onions (optional)

1 In a 3½- or 4-quart slow cooker, combine broth, uncooked wild rice, carrot, mushrooms, melted butter, marjoram, salt, and pepper.

2 Cover and cook on low-heat setting for 5 to 6 hours.

3 Turn off cooker. Stir in dried cherries, the ⅔ cup green onions, and the pecans. Cover and let stand for 10 minutes. Serve with a slotted spoon. If desired, garnish with additional green onions.

Nutrition facts per serving: 169 cal., 5 g total fat (1 g sat. fat), 4 mg chol., 423 mg sodium, 27 g carbo., 3 g fiber, 5 g pro.

delicious DESSERTS

Mixed Berry Cobbler, *recipe page 222*

apple BREAD

Slow cookers are made-to-order for steaming breads such as these fruit and nut loaves.

Prep: 20 minutes
Cook: 1¾ to 2 hours (high)
Cool: 10 minutes
Makes: 2 loaves (6 servings per loaf)

1	**cup all-purpose flour**
1½	**teaspoons baking powder**
1	**teaspoon apple pie spice**
¼	**teaspoon salt**
½	**cup packed brown sugar**
2	**tablespoons cooking oil or melted butter**
2	**eggs, lightly beaten**
½	**cup applesauce**
½	**cup chopped walnuts, toasted**
½	**cup warm water**

1 Grease two 1-pint, straight-sided, wide-mouth canning jars well; flour the greased jars. Set aside.

2 In a medium bowl, combine flour, baking powder, apple pie spice, and salt. Make a well in the center of the flour mixture; set aside.

3 In a small bowl, combine brown sugar, oil, eggs, and applesauce. Add applesauce mixture all at once to the flour mixture. Stir just until moistened. Stir in walnuts.

4 Divide mixture between the prepared canning jars. Cover the jars tightly with greased foil, greased sides in. Place the jars in a 4- to 6-quart slow cooker. Pour the warm water into the cooker around the jars.

5 Cover and cook on high-heat setting for 1¾ to 2 hours or until a long wooden skewer inserted near the center of each comes out clean.

6 Remove jars from cooker; place on a wire rack. Cool for 10 minutes. Carefully remove bread from jars. Serve warm.

Nutrition facts per serving: 146 cal., 7 g total fat (1 g sat. fat), 35 mg chol., 113 mg sodium, 20 g carbo., 1 g fiber, 3 g pro.

apple BETTY

Now this is comfort food—apples and apple butter simmered with brown sugar and cinnamon-raisin bread!

Prep: 25 minutes
Cook: 4 hours (low)
Stand: 30 minutes
Makes: 6 to 8 servings

Nonstick cooking spray

5 **tart cooking apples, peeled, cored, and sliced (5 cups)**

¾ **cup packed brown sugar**

⅔ **cup apple butter**

½ **cup water**

5 **cups soft cinnamon-raisin bread cut into ½-inch cubes (about 5 slices)**

⅓ **cup butter, melted**

Caramel ice cream topping and/or vanilla ice cream (optional)

1 Lightly coat a 3½- or 4-quart slow cooker with cooking spray; set aside.

2 In a large bowl, combine apples, brown sugar, apple butter, and the water. Toss until apples are coated. Place bread cubes in a medium bowl. Drizzle with melted butter, tossing until mixed.

3 Place half of the buttered bread cubes in prepared cooker. Pour all of the apple mixture over bread cubes. Sprinkle remaining bread cubes over the apple mixture in cooker.

4 Cover and cook on low-heat setting for 4 hours.

5 Turn off cooker. Let stand, uncovered, for 30 minutes to cool slightly before serving. If desired, top individual servings with caramel ice cream topping and/or vanilla ice cream.

Nutrition facts per serving: 492 cal., 12 g total fat (7 g sat. fat), 29 mg chol., 209 mg sodium, 97 g carbo., 5 g fiber, 2 g pro.

apple-cherry COBBLER

Triangles of refrigerated crescent rolls are baked ahead of time to place on top of each serving of this luscious apple and cherry cobbler.

Prep: 15 minutes
Cook: 5 to 6 hours (low) or
    2½ to 3 hours (high)
Makes: 6 to 8 servings

½ **cup sugar**

4 **teaspoons quick-cooking tapioca**

1 **teaspoon apple pie spice**

1½ **pounds cooking apples, peeled, cored, and cut into ½-inch-thick slices (4½ cups)**

1 **16-ounce can pitted tart red cherries, undrained**

½ **cup dried cherries**

Spiced Triangles*

Ice cream (such as butter pecan or cinnamon; optional)

❶ In a 3½- or 4-quart slow cooker, combine sugar, tapioca, and apple pie spice. Stir in apple slices, canned cherries, and dried cherries.

❷ Cover and cook on low-heat setting for 5 to 6 hours or on high-setting for 2½ to 3 hours.

❸ To serve, spoon the apple mixture into dessert dishes. Top with Spiced Triangles and, if desired, ice cream.

***Spiced Triangles:** Preheat oven to 375°F. In a small bowl, combine 1 tablespoon sugar and ½ teaspoon apple pie spice. Unroll one 8-ounce package (8) refrigerated crescent rolls. Separate triangles. Brush 1 tablespoon melted butter or margarine over dough triangles; lightly sprinkle with sugar mixture. Cut each triangle into three smaller triangles. Place on an ungreased baking sheet. Bake for 8 to 10 minutes or until bottoms are lightly browned. Transfer triangles to a wire rack and let cool. Makes 24 triangles.

Nutrition facts per serving: 414 cal., 10 g total fat (4 g sat. fat), 5 mg chol., 317 mg sodium, 79 g carbo., 5 g fiber, 7 g pro.

double-berry COBBLER

Prep: 25 minutes
Cook: 1¾ to 2 hours (high)
Stand: 1 hour
Makes: 6 servings

1 cup all-purpose flour

1¾ cup sugar

1 teaspoon baking powder

¼ teaspoon salt

¼ teaspoon ground cinnamon

¼ teaspoon ground nutmeg

2 eggs

3 tablespoons cooking oil

2 tablespoons milk

3 cups fresh blueberries or
 one 16-ounce bag frozen
 blueberries

3 cups fresh blackberries or
 one 16-ounce bag frozen
 blackberries

1 cup water

3 tablespoons quick-cooking
 tapioca

Vanilla ice cream (optional)

❶ In a medium bowl, stir together flour, the ¾ cup of the sugar, the baking powder, salt, cinnamon, and nutmeg. In a small bowl, beat eggs with a fork; stir in oil and milk. Add egg mixture to flour mixture; stir just until moistened. Set batter aside.

❷ In a large saucepan, combine blueberries, blackberries, the 1 cup remaining sugar, the water, and tapioca. Bring to boiling. Pour mixture into a 3½- or 4-quart slow cooker. Immediately spoon batter over mixture.

❸ Cover and cook on high-heat setting for 1¾ to 2 hours or until a toothpick inserted into the center of the topping comes out clean. Turn off cooker. Let stand for 1 hour to cool slightly before serving. If desired, serve with ice cream.

Nutrition facts per serving: 478 cal., 10 g total fat (2 g sat. fat), 71 mg chol., 194 mg sodium, 97 g carbo., 6 g fiber, 6 g pro.

pineapple-peach COBBLER

Pineapple and peaches simmer into a mellow fruit filling that's scrumptious beneath fluffy iced cinnamon rolls.

Prep: 15 minutes
Cook: 1½ hours (high),
　　　+ 1 hour
Stand: 30 minutes
Makes: 8 servings

Nonstick cooking spray

2　**21-ounce cans pineapple pie filling**

1　**6- or 7-ounce package dried peaches, snipped**

½　**cup orange juice**

1　**17.5-ounce package (5) refrigerated large cinnamon rolls**

Vanilla ice cream (optional)

1 Lightly coat a 3½- or 4-quart slow cooker with cooking spray. In the prepared cooker, combine pie filling, dried peaches, and orange juice.

2 Cover and cook on high-heat setting about 1½ hours or until fruit mixture is hot and bubbly.

3 Stir fruit mixture. Place cinnamon rolls on a cutting board, cinnamon sides up (set icing aside). Cut each roll in half to make two semicircles. Place roll halves on top of fruit mixture in cooker, cinnamon sides up.

4 Cover and cook for about 1 hour more or until rolls are fluffy all the way through.

5 Turn off cooker. Let stand, uncovered, for 30 to 45 minutes to cool slightly before serving. Spread icing over rolls. If desired, top individual servings with ice cream.

Nutrition facts per serving: 467 cal., 8 g total fat (2 g sat. fat), 0 mg chol., 493 mg sodium, 96 g carbo., 2 g fiber, 4 g pro.

mock CHERRIES JUBILEE

Prep: 15 minutes
Cook: 4 to 5 hours (high)
Makes: 8 servings

2 **16-ounce packages frozen unsweetened pitted tart red cherries**

½ **cup cherry cider, apple cider, or apple juice**

½ **cup packed brown sugar**

2 **tablespoons quick-cooking tapioca**

1 **vanilla bean, split lengthwise, or 2 teaspoons vanilla**

2 **to 3 tablespoons cherry or almond liqueur**

  Pound cake slices, angel food cake slices, or vanilla ice cream

  Whipped cream (optional)

1 In a 3½- or 4-quart slow cooker, combine frozen cherries, cider, brown sugar, tapioca, and vanilla bean, if using.

2 Cover and cook on high-heat setting for 4 to 5 hours. Remove and discard vanilla bean halves, if using, or stir in vanilla. Stir in liqueur. Spoon over cake slices or ice cream in bowls. If desired, top with whipped cream.

Nutrition facts per serving: 428 cal., 15 g total fat (9 g sat. fat), 166 mg chol., 307 mg sodium, 68 g carbo., 2 g fiber, 5 g pro.

almond GRANOLA-TOPPED DATES AND APPLESAUCE

If you have the time, be sure to make your own crunchy granola using the recipe below. Enjoy any leftovers for breakfast splashed with some milk.

Prep: 25 minutes
Cook: 5 to 6 hours (low) or
       2½ to 3 hours (high)
Makes: 10 servings

3½ to 4 pounds cooking apples
    (such as Granny Smith),
    peeled, cored, and cut into
    chunks

¼ cup orange juice

¼ cup apple juice or apple cider

½ cup packed brown sugar

1½ teaspoons apple pie spice

1 8-ounce package chopped
  dates or 1 cup dried cherries
  or raisins

⅔ cup Almond Granola* or
  purchased granola cereal

1 Place apples in a 4- to 6-quart slow cooker. Add orange juice, apple juice, brown sugar, and apple pie spice; toss to coat. Cover and cook on low-heat setting for 5 to 6 hours or on high-heat setting for 2½ to 3 hours (apples should be very tender).

2 Using a potato masher or an immersion blender, mash or blend apple mixture to desired consistency. Stir in dates. Serve warm topped with Almond Granola.

*Almond Granola: Preheat oven to 300°F. In a large bowl, combine 2 cups regular rolled oats, 1½ cups sliced almonds, ¼ cup toasted wheat germ, and 1 teaspoon ground cinnamon. In a small bowl, stir together ½ cup honey and 2 tablespoons butter, melted; stir honey mixture into oat mixture. Spread evenly in a greased 15x10x1-inch baking pan. Bake, uncovered, for 30 to 35 minutes or until lightly browned, stirring once. Transfer to and spread on a large piece of foil to cool. Store in an airtight container at room temperature for up to 1 week or place in a freezer container and freeze for up to 3 months. Makes 5 cups.

Nutrition facts per serving: 223 cal., 2 g total fat (0 g sat. fat), 1 mg chol., 9 mg sodium, 54 g carbo., 6 g fiber, 2 g pro.

semisweet-chocolate
BREAD PUDDING

Remember to plan for oven-drying the bread cubes for this bread pudding. It will become one of your favorites, especially when served warm with whipped cream.

Prep: 20 minutes
Cook: 2½ hours (low)
Stand: 30 minutes
Makes: 8 servings

Nonstick cooking spray

3 **cups milk**

¾ **cup semisweet chocolate pieces**

¾ **cup presweetened cocoa powder**

3 **eggs, lightly beaten**

5 **cups ½-inch cubes Hawaiian sweet bread or cinnamon swirl bread (no raisins), dried***

Whipped cream (optional)

Presweetened cocoa powder (optional)

1 Lightly coat the inside of a 3½- or 4-quart slow cooker with cooking spray.

2 In a medium saucepan, bring milk to simmering; remove from heat. Add chocolate and ¾ cup cocoa powder (do not stir); let stand for 5 minutes. Whisk until smooth; cool slightly (about 10 minutes). In a large bowl, whisk together the eggs and chocolate mixture. Gently stir in bread cubes. Spoon bread mixture into the prepared cooker.

3 Cover and cook on low-heat setting for about 2½ hours or until puffed and a knife inserted near center comes out clean (do not use high-heat setting). Turn off cooker. Let stand, uncovered, for 30 minutes (pudding will fall during cooling).

4 To serve, spoon warm pudding into dessert dishes. If desired, top each serving with whipped cream and sprinkle with presweetened cocoa powder.

*Test Kitchen Tip: To make dry bread cubes, spread fresh bread cubes in a single layer in a 15x10x1-inch baking pan. Bake, uncovered, in a 300°F oven for 10 to 15 minutes or until dry, stirring twice; cool.

Nutrition facts per serving: 360 cal., 12 g total fat (6 g sat. fat), 95 mg chol., 214 mg sodium, 62 g carbo., 4 g fiber, 9 g pro.

L

Leftovers, freezing, 134
Legumes. *See also* Beans
    Curried Split Pea Soup, 154, *155*
    Smoked Sausage-Lentil Soup, 149
Lentil-Smoked Sausage Soup, 149

M

Manhattan-Style Clam Chowder, 161
Maple-Ginger Sweet Potatoes, 194, *195*
Meat. *See* Beef; Meatballs; Pork
Meatballs
    Apricot-Glazed Ham Balls, 32
    Meatball Sliders, 30, *31*
    Plum-Good Sausage and Meatballs, 33
    Swedish Meatballs, 69
    Sweet, Hot, and Sour Meatballs, 29
Mediterranean Chicken, 101
Mexican Chocolate Bread Pudding, 219
Mexican-Stuffed Sweet Peppers, 53
Mixed Berry Cobbler, 222, *223*
Mocha Pudding Cake, Nutty, 218
Mock Cherries Jubilee, 214
Molasses Baked Beans, 185
Mole with Chicken and Rice, 124
Moroccan-Style Short Ribs, 64, *65*
Multigrain Pilaf, 200, *201*
Mushrooms
    Beef with Mushrooms, 78
    Chicken with Sourdough-Mushroom Stuffing, 112
    Coq au Vin Stew, 164, *165*
    Easy Beef Burgundy, 75
    Hash Browns with Garlic-Mushroom Sauce, 189
    Swedish Meatballs, 69
Mu Shu-Style Chicken, 129

N

New England Sweet Potato Soup, 160
Noodles
    Beef Lo Mein, 62, *63*
    Chicken Stroganoff, 120, *121*
    Saucy Pot Roast with Noodles, 51
North African Beef Stew, 58

Nuts. *See also* Almonds; Pecans
    Apple Bread, 208
    Caramel-Spiced Pears, 228
    Nutty Mocha Pudding Cake, 218

O

Oats. *See* Granola
Olives
    Greek Chicken with Couscous, 113
    Mediterranean Chicken, 101
    Moroccan-Style Short Ribs, 64, *65*
    Picadillo Dip, 18, *19*
    Spicy Sausage Pizza Dip, 20, *21*
Onions
    Balsamic Root Vegetables, 186, *187*
    Caramelized Onions and Potatoes, 190, *191*
    Coq au Vin Stew, 164, *165*
Orange Pudding Caramel Cake, 230, *231*

P

Parmesan Cheese Bread, 205
Parsnips
    Balsamic Root Vegetables, 186, *187*
    Pork with Parsnips and Pears, 90, *91*
Pasta and noodles
    Beef Lo Mein, 62, *63*
    Chicken Osso Buco, 108, *109*
    Chicken Stroganoff, 120, *121*
    Creamy Tortellini Soup, 162, *163*
    Greek Chicken with Couscous, 113
    Italian Chicken and Pasta, 107
    Moroccan-Style Short Ribs, 64, *65*
    Saucy Pot Roast with Noodles, 51
    Tex-Mex Mac and Cheese, 82, *83*
    Turkey and Pasta Primavera, 134, *135*
Peach-Glazed Pork Roast with Corn Bread Stuffing, 85
Peach-Pineapple Cobbler, 213
Pears
    Caramel-Spiced Pears, 228
    Fennel and Pear Chicken Thighs, 116, *117*
    Pork with Parsnips and Pears, 90, *91*

Pecans
    Five-Spice Pecans, 10
    Fruity Rice Pudding, 232, *233*
    Nutty Mocha Pudding Cake, 218
    Orange Pudding Caramel Cake, 230, *231*
    Wild Rice with Pecans and Cherries, 196, *197*
Peppers. *See also* Chile peppers
    Beef Fajitas, 54, *55*
    Chicken Tortilla Soup, 142, *143*
    Country Captain, 104, *105*
    Mexican-Stuffed Sweet Peppers, 53
    Pizza by the Yard, 22, *23*
    So-Easy Pepper Steak, 76, *77*
Picadillo Dip, 18, *19*
Pineapple-Peach Cobbler, 213
Pita Chips, 11
Pizza by the Yard, 22, *23*
Plum-Good Sausage and Meatballs, 33
Polenta
    Gorgonzola Polenta, 68
    Polenta with Ground Beef Ragoût, 48, *49*
    Southwestern Polenta with Corn and Chiles, 202, *203*
Pork. *See also* Bacon; Ham; Pork sausages
    Apricot Pulled Pork, 92
    Barbecue Pork Ribs, 84
    Curried Split Pea Soup, 154, *155*
    Flamin' Cajun Riblets, 25
    Georgia Peach Ribs, 24
    Hot Pepper Pork Sandwiches, 98, *99*
    Italian Pork with Mashed Sweet Potatoes, 86, *87*
    Peach-Glazed Pork Roast with Corn Bread Stuffing, 85
    Pork Chops with Orange-Dijon Sauce, 96
    Pork with Parsnips and Pears, 90, *91*
    Seeded Pork Roast, 97
    Sweet-Sour Pork Stew, 89
Pork sausages
    Black Bean and Kielbasa Soup, 153
    Pizza by the Yard, 22, *23*
    Plum-Good Sausage and Meatballs, 33

Potatoes, Sauerkraut, and Sausage
Supper, 94, *95*
Smoked Sausage-Lentil Soup, 149
Spicy Sausage Pizza Dip, 20, *21*
Sweet, Hot, and Sour Meatballs, 29
Texas Two-Step Stew, 88
Potatoes. *See also* Sweet potatoes
Balsamic Root Vegetables, 186, *187*
Caramelized Onions and Potatoes,
190, *191*
Chicken in Wine Sauce, 102, *103*
Easy Cheesy Potatoes, 192, *193*
Ham and Scalloped Potatoes, 93
Hash Browns with Garlic-Mushroom
Sauce, 189
Hot German-Style Potato Salad, 188
Potatoes, Sauerkraut, and Sausage
Supper, 94, *95*
Saucy Green Beans and Potatoes,
174, *175*
Smashed Potato Soup, 158, *159*
Super-Simple Beef Stew, 80, *81*
Poultry. *See* Chicken; Turkey
Pudding, bread
Mexican Chocolate Bread Pudding,
219
Semisweet-Chocolate Bread Pudding,
226, *227*
Pudding, Fruity Rice, 232, *233*
Pudding cakes
Brownie Pudding Cake, 217
Gingerbread Pudding Cake, 224, *225*
Nutty Mocha Pudding Cake, 218
Orange Pudding Caramel Cake,
230, *231*

R

Raisins
Gingerbread Pudding Cake, 224, *225*
Picadillo Dip, 18, *19*
Stuffed Apples, 229
Raspberry jam
Raspberry Fudgey Brownies, 216
Sweet and Smoky Chicken, 122
Ratatouille, 180, *181*

Rice
Chicken Jambalaya, 128
Creamy Wild Rice Pilaf, 198, *199*
Fruity Rice Pudding, 232, *233*
Mexican-Stuffed Sweet Peppers, 53
Mole with Chicken and Rice, 124
Multigrain Pilaf, 200, *201*
Savory Bean and Spinach Soup,
146, *147*
Texas Two-Step Stew, 88
Wild Rice and Chicken Soup, 150, *151*
Wild Rice with Pecans and Cherries,
196, *197*
Rich Beef and Barley Soup, 148
Round Steak with Herbs, 74
Russian Braised Brisket, 40, *41*

S

Salads
Green Chile Taco Salad, 125
Hot German-Style Potato Salad, 188
Sandwiches
Apricot Pulled Pork, 92
Crock of Reubens, 34, *35*
Hot Pepper Pork Sandwiches, 98, *99*
Italian Beef Sandwiches, 56, *57*
Sloppy Joes with a Kick, 72, *73*
Saucy Green Beans and Potatoes, 174,
175
Saucy Pot Roast with Noodles, 51
Saucy Succotash, 182, *183*
Sauerkraut
Crock of Reubens, 34, *35*
Potatoes, Sauerkraut, and Sausage
Supper, 94, *95*
Sausages. *See also* Pork sausages
Chicken Jambalaya, 128
Savory Bean and Spinach Soup, 146, *147*
Seafood
Cajun Spinach-Shrimp Dip, 17
Horseradish-Crab Dip, 16
Manhattan-Style Clam Chowder, 161
Seeded Pork Roast, 97
Semisweet-Chocolate Bread Pudding,
226, *227*
Sesame-Ginger Turkey Wraps, 132, *133*

Short Ribs over Gorgonzola Polenta, 68
Shrimp-Spinach Dip, Cajun, 17
Sloppy Joes with a Kick, 72, *73*
Slow-cooker basics, 6–7
Smashed Potato Soup, 158, *159*
Smoked Sausage-Lentil Soup, 149
Smoky Barbecued Beef Brisket, 42
So-Easy Pepper Steak, 76, *77*
Soups. *See also* Chili; Stews
Beef-Vegetable Soup, 140, *141*
Black Bean and Kielbasa Soup, 153
Chicken and Vegetable Bean Soup,
144, *145*
Chicken Tortilla Soup, 142, *143*
Creamy Tortellini Soup, 162, *163*
Curried Split Pea Soup, 154, *155*
French Country Soup, 139
Italian Vegetable Soup, 138
Manhattan-Style Clam Chowder, 161
New England Sweet Potato Soup,
160
Rich Beef and Barley Soup, 148
Savory Bean and Spinach Soup,
146, *147*
Smashed Potato Soup, 158, *159*
Smoked Sausage-Lentil Soup, 149
Southwestern Bean Soup, 156, *157*
Wild Rice and Chicken Soup,
150, *151*
Southwestern Bean Soup, 156, *157*
Southwestern Polenta with Corn and
Chiles, 202, *203*
Spicy Creamed Corn, 184
Spicy Sausage Pizza Dip, 20, *21*
Spicy Steak and Beans, 70, *71*
Spinach
Cajun Spinach-Shrimp Dip, 17
Creamy Tortellini Soup, 162, *163*
Savory Bean and Spinach Soup,
146, *147*
Spinach-Artichoke Dip with Blue
Cheese and Bacon, 14, *15*
Split Pea Soup, Curried, 154, *155*
Squash
Ratatouille, 180, *181*
White Bean and Toasted Cumin
Chili, 168

Stews. *See also* Chili
    Beef Goulash, 44, *45*
    Boeuf à la Bourguignonne, 38, *39*
    Brunswick Stew, 130
    Chicken and Dumplings, 110, *111*
    Coq au Vin Stew, 164, *165*
    Country Italian Beef, 43
    Easy Beef Burgundy, 75
    Gingered Beef and Vegetables, 60, *61*
    North African Beef Stew, 58
    Polenta with Ground Beef Ragoût,
      48, *49*
    Super-Simple Beef Stew, 80, *81*
    Sweet-Sour Pork Stew, 89
    Texas Two-Step Stew, 88
Stuffed Apples, 229
Succotash, Saucy, 182, *183*
Super-Simple Beef Stew, 80, *81*
Swedish Meatballs, 69
Sweet, Hot, and Sour Meatballs, 29
Sweet and Smoky Chicken, 122
Sweet potatoes
    Italian Pork with Mashed Sweet
      Potatoes, 86, *87*
    Maple-Ginger Sweet Potatoes,
      194, *195*
    New England Sweet Potato Soup, 160
    North African Beef Stew, 58
Sweet-Sour Pork Stew, 89

T

Teriyaki and Orange Chicken, 126, *127*
Texas Two-Step Stew, 88
Tex-Mex Mac and Cheese, 82, *83*
Three-Bean Vegetarian Chili, 166, *167*

Thyme and Garlic Chicken, 100
Tomatoes
    Ginger-Tomato Chicken, 106
    Greek Chicken with Couscous, 113
    health benefits, 101
    Manhattan-Style Clam Chowder, 161
    Spicy Sausage Pizza Dip, 20, *21*
Tortillas
    Beef Fajitas, 54, *55*
    Chicken Tortilla Soup, 142, *143*
    Mu Shu-Style Chicken, 129
    Sesame-Ginger Turkey Wraps,
      132, *133*
Turkey
    Chicken Jambalaya, 128
    Green Chile Taco Salad, 125
    Sesame-Ginger Turkey Wraps,
      132, *133*
    Turkey and Pasta Primavera, 134, *135*
    Turkey Chablis, 131

V

Vegetables. *See also specific vegetables*
    Balsamic Root Vegetables, 186, *187*
    Beef Lo Mein, 62, *63*
    Beef-Vegetable Soup, 140, *141*
    Chicken and Vegetable Bean Soup,
      144, *145*
    Chicken and Vegetables with Herbs,
      114, *115*
    Italian Vegetable Soup, 138
    Teriyaki and Orange Chicken, 126, *127*
    Turkey and Pasta Primavera, 134, *135*
    Vegetable and Garbanzo Curry,
      178, *179*

W

White beans
    Chicken and Vegetable Bean Soup,
      144, *145*
    Chicken Chili, 152
    French Country Soup, 139
    Green Chile Taco Salad, 125
    Savory Bean and Spinach Soup,
      146, *147*
    White Bean and Toasted Cumin
      Chili, 168
    White Bean Spread, 11
Wild rice
    Creamy Wild Rice Pilaf, 198, *199*
    Multigrain Pilaf, 200, *201*
    Wild Rice and Chicken Soup, 150, *151*
    Wild Rice with Pecans and Cherries,
      196, *197*
Wine, cooking with, 75